中图e码使用说明

中图e码是中国图书进出口公司应用先进数字印刷技术制作的条码，该码为每本正版图书赋予独一无二的"二维码身份证"。

下载音频操作步骤：

1. 微信绑定

使用微信对"中图e码"进行扫描，并且点击"确定"，授权该帐号与本人微信帐号实现绑定。

2. 关注公众号

使用同一个微信帐号扫描并关注以下"中图e码"微信公众号，点击界面下方"e码资源"，即可查看，并在线反复播放所有已绑定书籍的音视频。

温馨提示：试听耗费流量，建议在wifi环境下使用。

3. 如需下载重复收听，请登陆网址：

http://www.chinapod.cn

点击网页右上方"登录"，使用微信扫描"中图e码"，选择"登录"。

W9-CBW-051

新东方雅思
专业，为我

扫码关注"新东方留学考试学习平台"微信订阅号，获取最新留学考试资讯和新东方独家备考资料。

新东方留学考试
学习平台

剑桥雅思官方指南
（附DVD-ROM）

当当购买

京东购买

提示

购买此书后，请沿左侧
虚线撕开，按照"中图
e码使用说明"获取本
书配套音频。

【版权所有，侵权必究】

CAMBRIDGE
UNIVERSITY PRESS

CAMBRIDGE ENGLISH
Language Assessment
Part of the University of Cambridge

Cambridge English

OFFICIAL

IELTS12
GENERAL TRAINING

WITH ANSWERS

AUTHENTIC EXAMINATION PAPERS

Cambridge University Press
www.cambridge.org/elt

Cambridge English Language Assessment
www.cambridgeenglish.org

Information on this title: www.cambridge.org/9781316637838

© Cambridge University Press and UCLES 2017

First published 2017

20 19 18 17 16 15 14 13 12 11 10 9 8 7 6 5 4 3 2 1

Printed in China by CNPIEC Beijing Congreat Printing Co., Ltd.

A catalogue record for this publication is available from the British Library

ISBN 978-1-108-40972-8 General Training Student's Book with answers with Audio
China reprint edition
ISBN 978-1-316-63783-8 General Training Student's Book with answers
ISBN 978-1-316-63787-6 General Training Student's Book with answers with Audio
ISBN 978-1-108-40966-7 Academic Student's Book with answers with Audio
New Oriental School China reprint edition
ISBN 978-108-40963-6 Academic Student's Book with answers with Audio
China reprint edition
ISBN 978-1-316-63782-1 Academic Student's Book with answers
ISBN 978-1-316-63786-9 Academic Student's Book with answers with Audio
ISBN 978-1-316-63784-5 Audio CDs (2)

Contents

Introduction

The International English Language Testing System (IELTS) is widely recognised as a reliable means of assessing the language ability of candidates who need to study or work where English is the language of communication. These Practice Tests are designed to give future IELTS candidates an idea of whether their English is at the required level.

IELTS is owned by three partners, Cambridge English Language Assessment, part of the University of Cambridge, the British Council and IDP Education Pty Limited (through its subsidiary company, IELTS Australia Pty Limited). Further information on IELTS can be found on the IELTS website www.ielts.org.

WHAT IS THE TEST FORMAT?

IELTS consists of four components. All candidates take the same Listening and Speaking tests. There is a choice of Reading and Writing tests according to whether a candidate is taking the Academic or General Training module.

Academic	General Training
For candidates wishing to study at undergraduate or postgraduate levels, and for those seeking professional registration.	For candidates wishing to migrate to an English-speaking country (Australia, Canada, New Zealand, UK), and for those wishing to train or study at below degree level.

The test components are taken in the following order:

Listening		
4 sections, 40 items, approximately 30 minutes		
Academic Reading 3 sections, 40 items 60 minutes	or	**General Training Reading** 3 sections, 40 items 60 minutes
Academic Writing 2 tasks 60 minutes	or	**General Training Writing** 2 tasks 60 minutes
Speaking 11 to 14 minutes		
Total Test Time 2 hours 44 minutes		

GENERAL TRAINING TEST FORMAT

Listening

This test consists of four sections, each with ten questions. The first two sections are concerned with social needs. The first section is a conversation between two speakers and the second section is a monologue. The final two sections are concerned with situations related to educational or training contexts. The third section is a conversation between up to four people and the fourth section is a monologue.

A variety of question types is used, including: multiple choice, matching, plan/map/ diagram labelling, form completion, note completion, table completion, flow-chart completion, summary completion, sentence completion and short-answer questions.

Candidates hear the recording once only and answer the questions as they listen. Ten minutes are allowed at the end for candidates to transfer their answers to the answer sheet.

Reading

This test consists of three sections with 40 questions. The texts are taken from notices, advertisements, leaflets, newspapers, instruction manuals, books and magazines. The first section contains texts relevant to basic linguistic survival in English, with tasks mainly concerned with providing factual information. The second section focuses on the work context and involves texts of more complex language. The third section involves reading more extended texts, with a more complex structure, but with the emphasis on descriptive and instructive rather than argumentative texts.

A variety of question types is used, including: multiple choice, identifying information (True/False/Not Given), identifying the writer's views/claims (Yes/No/Not Given), matching information, matching headings, matching features, matching sentence endings, sentence completion, summary completion, note completion, table completion, flow-chart completion, diagram label completion and short-answer questions.

Writing

This test consists of two tasks. It is suggested that candidates spend about 20 minutes on Task 1, which requires them to write at least 150 words, and 40 minutes on Task 2, which requires them to write at least 250 words. Task 2 contributes twice as much as Task 1 to the Writing score.

In Task 1, candidates are asked to respond to a given situation with a letter requesting information or explaining the situation. They are assessed on their ability to engage in personal correspondence, elicit and provide general factual information, express needs, wants, likes and dislikes, express opinions, complaints, etc.

In Task 2, candidates are presented with a point of view, argument or problem. They are assessed on their ability to provide general factual information, outline a problem and present a solution, present and justify an opinion, and to evaluate and challenge ideas, evidence or arguments.

Candidates are also assessed on their ability to write in an appropriate style.

More information on assessing the Writing test, including Writing assessment criteria (public version), is available on the IELTS website.

Speaking

This test takes between 11 and 14 minutes and is conducted by a trained examiner. There are three parts:

Part 1

The candidate and the examiner introduce themselves. Candidates then answer general questions about themselves, their home/family, their job/studies, their interests and a wide range of similar familiar topic areas. This part lasts between four and five minutes.

Part 2

The candidate is given a task card with prompts and is asked to talk on a particular topic. The candidate has one minute to prepare and they can make some notes if they wish, before speaking for between one and two minutes. The examiner then asks one or two questions on the same topic.

Part 3

The examiner and the candidate engage in a discussion of more abstract issues which are thematically linked to the topic in Part 2. The discussion lasts between four and five minutes.

The Speaking test assesses whether candidates can communicate effectively in English. The assessment takes into account Fluency and Coherence, Lexical Resource, Grammatical Range and Accuracy, and Pronunciation. More information on assessing the Speaking test, including Speaking assessment criteria (public version), is available on the IELTS website.

HOW IS IELTS SCORED?

IELTS results are reported on a nine-band scale. In addition to the score for overall language ability, IELTS provides a score in the form of a profile for each of the four skills (Listening, Reading, Writing and Speaking). These scores are also reported on a nine-band scale. All scores are recorded on the Test Report Form along with details of the candidate's nationality, first language and date of birth. Each Overall Band Score corresponds to a descriptive statement which gives a summary of the English language ability of a candidate classified at that level. The nine bands and their descriptive statements are as follows:

9 Expert User – *Has fully operational command of the language: appropriate, accurate and fluent with complete understanding.*

8 Very Good User – *Has fully operational command of the language with only occasional unsystematic inaccuracies and inappropriacies. Misunderstandings may occur in unfamiliar situations. Handles complex detailed argumentation well.*

7 Good User – *Has operational command of the language, though with occasional inaccuracies, inappropriacies and misunderstandings in some situations. Generally handles complex language well and understands detailed reasoning.*

6 Competent User – *Has generally effective command of the language despite some inaccuracies, inappropriacies and misunderstandings. Can use and understand fairly complex language, particularly in familiar situations.*

5 Modest User – *Has partial command of the language, coping with overall meaning in most situations, though is likely to make many mistakes. Should be able to handle basic communication in own field.*

4 Limited User – *Basic competence is limited to familiar situations. Has frequent problems in understanding and expression. Is not able to use complex language.*

3 Extremely Limited User – *Conveys and understands only general meaning in very familiar situations. Frequent breakdowns in communication occur.*

2 Intermittent User – *No real communication is possible except for the most basic information using isolated words or short formulae in familiar situations and to meet immediate needs. Has great difficulty understanding spoken and written English.*

1 Non User – *Essentially has no ability to use the language beyond possibly a few isolated words.*

0 Did not attempt the test – *No assessable information provided.*

MARKING THE PRACTICE TESTS

Listening and Reading

The Answer Keys are on pages 123–130.
Each question in the Listening and Reading tests is worth one mark.

Questions which require letter / Roman numeral answers
- For questions where the answers are letters or Roman numerals, you should write *only* the number of answers required. For example, if the answer is a single letter or numeral you should write only one answer. If you have written more letters or numerals than are required, the answer must be marked wrong.

Questions which require answers in the form of words or numbers
- Answers may be written in upper or lower case.
- Words in brackets are *optional* – they are correct, but not necessary.
- Alternative answers are separated by a slash (/).
- If you are asked to write an answer using a certain number of words and/or (a) number(s), you will be penalised if you exceed this. For example, if a question specifies an answer using NO MORE THAN THREE WORDS and the correct answer is 'black leather coat', the answer 'coat of black leather' is *incorrect*.
- In questions where you are expected to complete a gap, you should only transfer the necessary missing word(s) onto the answer sheet. For example, to complete 'in the …', where the correct answer is 'morning', the answer 'in the morning' would be *incorrect*.
- All answers require correct spelling (including words in brackets).
- Both US and UK spelling are acceptable and are included in the Answer Key.
- All standard alternatives for numbers, dates and currencies are acceptable.
- All standard abbreviations are acceptable.
- You will find additional notes about individual answers in the Answer Key.

Writing

The sample answers are on pages 131–138. It is not possible for you to give yourself a mark for the Writing tasks. We have provided sample answers (written by candidates), showing their score and the examiner's comments. These sample answers will give you an insight into what is required for the Writing test.

HOW SHOULD YOU INTERPRET YOUR SCORES?

At the end of each Listening and Reading Answer Key you will find a chart which will help you assess whether, on the basis of your Practice Test results, you are ready to take the IELTS test.

In interpreting your score, there are a number of points you should bear in mind. Your performance in the real IELTS test will be reported in two ways: there will be a Band Score from 1 to 9 for each of the components and an Overall Band Score from 1 to 9, which is the average of your scores in the four components. However, institutions considering your application are advised to look at both the Overall Band Score and the Bands for each component in order to determine whether you have the language skills needed for a particular course of study or work environment. For example, if you are applying for a course which involves a lot of reading and writing, but no lectures, listening skills might be less important and a score of 5 in Listening might be acceptable if the Overall Band Score was 7. However, for a course which has lots of lectures and spoken instructions, a score of 5 in Listening might be unacceptable even though the Overall Band Score was 7.

Once you have marked your tests, you should have some idea of whether your listening and reading skills are good enough for you to try the IELTS test. If you did well enough in one component, but not in others, you will have to decide for yourself whether you are ready to take the test.

The Practice Tests have been checked to ensure that they are of approximately the same level of difficulty as the real IELTS test. However, we cannot guarantee that your score in the Practice Tests will be reflected in the real IELTS test. The Practice Tests can only give you an idea of your possible future performance and it is ultimately up to you to make decisions based on your score.

Different institutions accept different IELTS scores for different types of courses. We have based our recommendations on the average scores which the majority of institutions accept. The institution to which you are applying may, of course, require a higher or lower score than most other institutions.

Further information

For more information about IELTS or any other Cambridge English Language Assessment examination, write to:

Cambridge English Language Assessment
1 Hills Road
Cambridge
CB1 2EU
United Kingdom

https://support.cambridgeenglish.org
http://www.ielts.org

Test 5

SECTION 1   Questions 1–10

Complete the notes below.

*Write **ONE WORD AND/OR A NUMBER** for each answer.*

Family Excursions

Cruise on a lake

Example

- Travel on an old ......*steamship*......

- Can take photos of the **1** .... that surround the lake

Farm visit

- Children can help feed the sheep
- Visit can include a 40-minute ride on a **2** ....
- Visitors can walk in the farm's **3** .... by the lake
- **4** .... is available at extra cost

Cycling trips

- Cyclists explore the Back Road
- A **5** .... is provided
- Only suitable for cyclists who have some **6** ....
  - Bikes can be hired from **7** .... (near the Cruise Ship terminal)

- Cyclists need:
    - a repair kit
    - food and drink
    - a **8** .... (can be hired)
- There are no **9** .... or accommodation in the area

Cost

- Total cost for whole family of cruise and farm visit: **10** $ ....

SECTION 2   *Questions 11–20*

Questions 11–14

*Choose the correct letter, **A**, **B** or **C**.*

Talk to new kitchen assistants

11   According to the manager, what do most people like about the job of kitchen assistant?

    A   the variety of work
    B   the friendly atmosphere
    C   the opportunities for promotion

12   The manager is concerned about some of the new staff's

    A   jewellery.
    B   hair styles.
    C   shoes.

13   The manager says that the day is likely to be busy for kitchen staff because

    A   it is a public holiday.
    B   the head chef is absent.
    C   the restaurant is almost fully booked.

14   Only kitchen staff who are 18 or older are allowed to use

    A   the waste disposal unit.
    B   the electric mixer.
    C   the meat slicer.

Questions 15 and 16

*Choose **TWO** letters, **A–E**.*

According to the manager, which **TWO** things can make the job of kitchen assistant stressful?

    A   They have to follow orders immediately.
    B   The kitchen gets very hot.
    C   They may not be able to take a break.
    D   They have to do overtime.
    E   The work is physically demanding.

Questions 17–20

What is the responsibility of each of the following restaurant staff?

*Choose **FOUR** answers from the box and write the correct letter, **A–F**, next to Questions 17–20.*

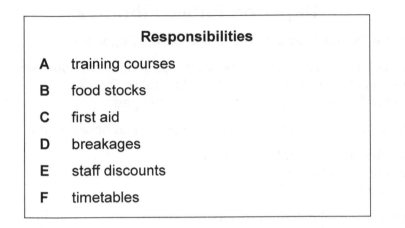

Responsibilities
A training courses
B food stocks
C first aid
D breakages
E staff discounts
F timetables

Restaurant staff

17 Joy Parkins ....

18 David Field ....

19 Dexter Wills ....

20 Mike Smith ....

SECTION 3   *Questions 21–30*

Questions 21–23

Choose the correct letter, A, B or C.

Paper on Public Libraries

21   What will be the main topic of Trudie and Stewart's paper?

    A   how public library services are organised in different countries
    B   how changes in society are reflected in public libraries
    C   how the funding of public libraries has changed

22   They agree that one disadvantage of free digitalised books is that

    A   they may take a long time to read.
    B   they can be difficult to read.
    C   they are generally old.

23   Stewart expects that in the future libraries will

    A   maintain their traditional function.
    B   become centres for local communities.
    C   no longer contain any books.

Questions 24–30

Complete the notes below.

*Write **ONE WORD ONLY** for each answer.*

Study of local library: possible questions

- whether it has a **24** .... of its own

- its policy regarding noise of various kinds

- how it's affected by laws regarding all aspects of **25** ....

- how the design needs to take the **26** .... of customers into account

- what **27** .... is required in case of accidents

- why a famous person's **28** .... is located in the library

- whether it has a **29** .... of local organisations

- how it's different from a library in a **30** ....

SECTION 4   *Questions 31–40*

Complete the notes below.

*Write **NO MORE THAN TWO WORDS** for each answer.*

Four business values

Many business values can result in **31** ....

Senior managers need to understand and deal with the potential
32 .... that may result.

Collaboration

During a training course, the speaker was in a team that had to build
a **33** ....

Other teams experienced **34** .... from trying to collaborate.

The speaker's team won because they reduced collaboration.

Sales of a **35** .... were poor because of collaboration.

Industriousness

Hard work may be a bad use of various company **36** ....

The word 'lazy' in this context refers to people who avoid doing tasks that
are **37** ....

Creativity

An advertising campaign for a **38** .... was memorable but failed
to boost sales.

Creativity should be used as a response to a particular **39** ....

Excellence

According to one study, on average, pioneers had a **40** .... that was
far higher than that of followers.

Companies that always aim at excellence may miss opportunities.

READING

SECTION 1   *Questions 1–14*

Read the text below and answer Questions 1–8.

A   Bath International Music Festival

From electronic to folk, jazz and classical, this festival is renowned for bringing world-class musicians to this historical city. Starting with a great night of free music, 'Party in the City' this year is going to be no exception.

B   The Great Escape

Often referred to as Europe's leading festival for new music, more than 300 bands will perform to around 10,000 people in 30-plus venues, meaning you're sure to see the next big thing in music.

C   Springwatch Festival

The much loved television series *Springwatch* celebrates the countryside as it does every year, with sheep herding, wood carving demonstrations, insect hunts and more activities, accompanied by live music and a great farmers' market, offering all sorts of mouth-watering produce.

D   Wychwood Music Festival

Rightly nominated for the best family festival award every year since it began in 2005, this festival offers a combination of different music genres – many featuring artists from around the Wychwood area – and comedy, alongside a selection of outdoor cafés serving amazing world foods.

E   Love Food Festival

Bringing together a selection of the finest produce, this festival aims to educate visitors about how food should be produced and where it should come from, through sampling a range of tasty treats, cooked on site.

F   The 3 Wishes Faery Festival

The UK's most magical event, this is a three-day festival of folk art, live music and fashion shows set in the beautiful wild surroundings of Bodmin Moor. If you don't fancy taking a tent, some local residents usually offer to put visitors up.

G   Bath International Dance Festival

Featuring demonstrations from world champion dancers and stars from the TV series *Strictly Come Dancing*, the festival promises toe-tapping action, including a world-record attempt, where everyone is invited to join in.

Questions 1–8

*Look at the seven advertisements for festivals in the UK, **A–G**, on page 16.*

For which festival are the following statements true?

*Write the correct letter, **A–G**, in boxes 1–8 on your answer sheet.*

NB *You may use any letter more than once.*

1   Visitors can help to make one particular event a success at this festival.

2   People can listen to local musicians here.

3   At this festival, people can listen to music in lots of different places.

4   It is not necessary to pay for one of the events here.

5   It is possible to stay overnight at this festival.

6   Children will enjoy this festival.

7   Visitors can get advice here.

8   People can watch craftspeople at work here.

Read the text below and answer Questions 9–14.

BIG ROCK CLIMBING CENTRE

Big Rock Climbing Centre is a modern, friendly, professionally run centre offering over 1,250 square metres of fantastic indoor climbing. We use trained and experienced instructors to give you the opportunity to learn and develop climbing skills, keep fit and have fun. Master our 11 m-high climbing walls, using a rope harness, for an unbeatable sense of achievement. Or experience the thrills of climbing without any harness in our special low-level arena, which has foam mats on the floor to cushion any fall safely.

Who is Big Rock for?

Almost anyone can enjoy Big Rock. Previous climbing experience and specialist equipment are not required. You can come on your own or with friends and family. Come as a fun alternative to the gym or for a special day out with the kids. If you're visiting with friends or family but not climbing, or just fancy coming to look, please feel free to relax in our excellent café overlooking the climbing areas.

Mobile Climbing Wall

Available on a day hire basis at any location, the Big Rock Mobile Climbing Wall is the perfect way to enhance any show, festival or event. The mobile wall can be used indoors or outdoors and features four unique 7.3 m-high climbing faces designed to allow four people to climb simultaneously. Quick to set up and pack up, the Mobile Climbing Wall is staffed by qualified and experienced climbing instructors, providing the opportunity to climb the wall in a controlled and safe environment. When considering what to wear, we've found that trousers and t-shirts are ideal. We will, however, ask people to remove scarves. Most flat shoes are suitable as long as they're enclosed and support the foot. The mobile wall is very adaptable and can be operated in light rain and winds up to 50 kph. There are, however, particular measures that we take in such conditions.

What about hiring the Mobile Climbing Wall for my school or college?

As climbing is different from the usual team games practised at schools, we've found that some students who don't usually like participating in sports are willing to have a go on the mobile climbing wall. If you're concerned that some children may not want to take part because they feel nervous if they climb, then please be assured that our instructors will support them up to a level which they're comfortable with. They will still benefit greatly from the experience.

Questions 9–14

Do the following statements agree with the information given in the text on page 18?

In boxes 9–14 on your answer sheet, write

> **TRUE**   *if the statement agrees with the information*
> **FALSE**   *if the statement contradicts the information*
> **NOT GIVEN** *if there is no information on this*

9   When climbing at the Big Rock Centre, it is compulsory to be attached by a rope.

10 People who just want to watch the climbing can enter the Centre without paying.

11 People can arrange to have a climbing session in their own garden if they wish.

12 A certain item of clothing is forbidden for participants.

13 The Mobile Climbing Wall can only be used in dry, calm weather.

14 It is inadvisable for children who are afraid of heights to use the Mobile Climbing Wall.

SECTION 2   *Questions 15–27*

Read the text below and answer Questions 15–20.

Marketing advice for new businesses

If you're setting up your own business, here's some advice on getting customers.

Know where your customers look

Your customers aren't necessarily where you think they are. So if you're advertising where they're just not looking, it's wasted money. That's why it pays to do a bit of research. Every time someone contacts your company, ask them where they found out about you. And act on this information so you're advertising in the right places.

Always think like a customer

What makes your customers tick? Find out, and you're halfway to saying the right things in your advertising. So take the time to ask them. A simple phone or email survey of your own customers, politely asking why they use you, what they really like and what they don't, is invaluable.

Make sure customers know you're there

If a customer can't see you, they can't buy from you. There are loads of opportunities to promote your business – print, press, direct mail, telemarketing, email and the internet – and using a mix of these increases your chances of being seen (and remembered).

Ignore your customers and they'll go away

It sounds obvious, but companies who talk to their customers have much better retention rates than those that don't, so it's worth staying in touch. Capture your customers' email addresses upfront. Follow up a transaction to check they're happy with the service and, if possible, send them updates that are helpful, informative and relevant.

Know what works (and what doesn't)

Do what the professionals do, and measure all your advertising. That'll tell you what you're doing right – and where there's room for improvement. You never know, it might just throw up some information that could change your business for the better.

Remember word-of-mouth: the best advertising there is

A recent survey found that consumers are 50% more likely to be influenced by word-of-mouth recommendations than by TV or radio ads. So your reputation is your greatest asset. If your current customers are impressed with your company, they'll be more inclined to recommend you to others. On the flip side, if they experience bad service they probably won't complain to you – but you can be sure they will to their friends.

Questions 15–20

Complete the sentences below.

*Choose **ONE WORD ONLY** from the text for each answer.*

Write your answers in boxes 15–20 on your answer sheet.

15 Some .... will help you to discover the most effective places to advertise.

16 A .... of your customers will show you how they feel about your company.

17 A .... of forms of advertising will make it more likely that potential customers will find out about you.

18 If you can, provide customers with useful .... about your business.

19 Measuring the effects of your advertising can give you .... that will improve your business.

20 Success in finding new customers largely depends on your ....

Read the text below and answer Questions 21–27.

Working Time Regulations for Mobile Workers

These rules apply to drivers and crew of heavy goods vehicles or public service vehicles. The rules limit the amount of time that can be worked.

Those defined in the Regulations as being self-employed are currently not covered by the Regulations.

What are the limits?

- An average of 48 hours' work per week.
- In any single week up to 60 hours can be worked so long as the 48-hour average is maintained.
- Night work is limited to 10 hours per night, unless there is a workforce agreement to work longer.
- Statutory annual leave and any sick leave and/or maternity/paternity leave counts as working time.

What counts as work?

In general, any activities performed in connection with the transport operation count as work, for example, driving, loading/unloading and those checks that are the responsibility of drivers, such as checking lights, brakes, etc. There are a number of periods of time that do not count as work, for example, travelling between home and your normal place of work, lunch or other breaks and periods of availability.

Periods of availability are periods of time during which the mobile worker is not required to remain at their workstation but is required to be available for work, the foreseeable duration of which is known about in advance, for example:

- Delays at a distribution centre.
- Reporting for work then being informed that no duties are to be undertaken for a specified period.
- Accompanying a vehicle being transported, for example by train.

A period of availability can be taken at the workstation. Providing the worker has a reasonable amount of freedom (e.g. they can read and relax) for a known duration, this could satisfy the requirements of a period of availability.

Situations when a period of time should not be recorded as a period of availability:

- Hold-ups due to congestion, because the driver would be stopping and starting the vehicle.
- Frequently moving up within a queue (e.g. waiting within a queue to load or unload) every other minute.

Questions 21–27

Complete the notes below.

*Choose **ONE WORD ONLY** from the text for each answer.*

Write your answers in boxes 21–27 on your answer sheet.

Working Time Regulations for Mobile Workers

These apply to people working on lorries, buses, etc.

They don't apply to **21** .... workers.

Maximum working hours: 60 hours a week, provided the **22** .... is no more than 48 hours.

Night work can be more than 10 hours with the **23** .... of the workers.

Work includes driving, loading and unloading, and carrying out various **24** .... of the vehicle.

Periods of availability include:

    going on a **25** .... or other form of transport with a vehicle

    a period at the workstation when the driver has some **26** .... might count as a period of availability

Periods of availability exclude:

    time spent stopping and starting the vehicle when **27** .... causes delays

    being in a queue, e.g. in order to load or unload

SECTION 3   *Questions 28–40*

Read the text below and answer Questions 28–40.

A brief history of automata

An automaton is a machine, usually made to resemble a person or animal, that operates on its own, once it has been started. Although few are constructed nowadays, they have a history stretching back well over two thousand years. Several myths show that the ancient Greeks were interested in the creation of automata. In one, Hephaestus, the god of all mechanical arts, was reputed to have made two female statues of pure gold which assisted him and accompanied him wherever he went. As well as giving automata a place in mythology, the Greeks almost certainly created some. These were probably activated by levers and powered by human action, although there are descriptions of steam and water being used as sources of power. Automata were sometimes intended as toys, or as tools for demonstrating basic scientific principles.

Other ancient cultures, too, seem to have developed automata. In Egypt, Ctesibius experimented with air pressure and pneumatic principles. One of his creations was a singing blackbird powered by water. A Chinese text of the third century BC describes a life-size, human-shaped figure that could walk rapidly, move its head up and down, sing and wink its eye.

Much later, Arab engineers of the ninth and thirteenth centuries wrote detailed treatises on how to build programmable musical fountains, mechanical servants, and elaborate clocks. A ninth-century ruler in Baghdad had a silver and gold tree with metal birds that sang. The art of creating automata developed considerably during the fifteenth century, linked with improvements in clock making: the mechanisms of automata and clocks had a great deal in common. Some truly remarkable automata were produced at this time. Muller was reputed to have made an artificial eagle which flew to greet the Emperor on his entry into Nuremberg, Germany, in 1470, then returned to perch on top of a city gate and, by stretching its wings and bowing, saluted the emperor on his arrival. Leonardo da Vinci made a lion in honour of the king of France, which advanced towards him, stopped, opened its chest with a claw and pointed to the French coat of arms.

Automata were normally very expensive toys for the very rich. They were made for royal or aristocratic patrons, to be viewed only by themselves and selected guests – who were expected to be impressed by their wealth. Automata were also created for public show, however, and many appeared on clock towers, such as the one in Bern, Switzerland, built in 1530.

During the eighteenth century, some watchmakers made automata to contribute to the progress of medicine and the natural sciences, particularly to investigate the mechanical laws governing the structure and movement of living things. Many of their creations simulated almost perfectly the complex structure of human beings and animals. Maillardet made extensive use of gearing and cogs to produce automata of horses, worked by turning a handle. Vaucanson produced a duck made of gilded copper which ate, drank and quacked like a real duck. He also made a life-size female flute player. Air passes through the complex mechanism, causing the lips and fingers of the player to move naturally on the flute, opening and closing holes on it. This automaton had a repertoire of twelve tunes.

In another well-known piece, Merlin's silver swan made in 1773, the swan sits in a stream consisting of glass rods where small silver fish are swimming. When the clockwork is wound, a music box plays and the glass rods rotate, giving the impression of a flowing stream. The swan turns its head from side to side. It soon notices the fish and bends down to catch and eat one, then raises its head to the upright position. The mechanism still works.

One of the most skilled makers of automata was the Swiss watchmaker Jaquet-Droz. He produced three automata which, even today, are considered wonders of science and mechanical engineering. One of these, The Writer, simulates a boy sitting at a desk, dipping his pen into the ink and writing perfectly legibly.

Another stunning creation of the eighteenth century was the Mechanical Theatre in the grounds of Austria's Hellbrunn Palace, home of the Archbishop of Salzburg. Designed by the miner Rosenegger, and completed in 1752, this depicts the nobility's idea of a perfect society, with every class in its proper place. The figures inside a palace depict eighteenth-century court life, while industrious activity is carried on in and around this building. A total of 141 mobile and 52 immobile little figures demonstrate all manner of trades of the period: building workers bring materials to the foreman, who drinks; butchers slaughter an ox; a barber shaves a man. A dancing bear performs, guards march past the palace, a farmer pushes an old woman in a wheelbarrow over the road. The theatre shows great skill in clock making and water technology, consisting of hidden waterwheels, copper wiring and cogwheels.

During the nineteenth century, mass production techniques meant that automata could be made cheaply and easily, and they became toys for children rather than an expensive adult amusement. Between 1860 and 1910, small family businesses in Paris made thousands of clockwork automata and mechanical singing birds and exported them around the world. However, the twentieth century saw traditional forms of automata fall out of favour.

Questions 28–30

Complete the summary below.

*Choose **ONE WORD ONLY** from the text for each answer.*

Write your answers in boxes 28–30 on your answer sheet.

Automata and the ancient Greeks

The ancient Greeks had a number of **28** .... concerning automata. According to one, the god Hephaestus created two assistants made of gold. The Greeks probably also created real automata; it seems most likely that the mechanism which controlled them consisted of **29** .... which were worked by human operators. Some automata were designed to be **30** .... with an educational purpose.

Questions 31–35

Look at the following descriptions (Questions 31–35) and the list of people below.

*Match each statement with the correct person, **A–G**.*

*Write the correct letter, **A–G**, in boxes 31–35 on your answer sheet.*

List of Descriptions

31 created an automaton that represented a bird in water, interacting with its surroundings

32 created an automaton that performed on a musical instrument

33 produced documents about how to create automata

34 created automata which required a human being to operate the mechanism

35 used air and water power

	List of People
A	Ctesibius
B	Arab engineers
C	da Vinci
D	Maillardet
E	Vaucanson
F	Merlin
G	Jaquet-Droz

Questions 36–40

Complete the sentences below.

*Choose **ONE WORD ONLY** from the text for each answer.*

Write your answers in boxes 36–40 on your answer sheet.

36   The Mechanical Theatre shows court life inside a ....

37   In the Mechanical Theatre, building workers, butchers and a barber represent various .... of the time.

38   .... provides the power that operates the Mechanical Theatre.

39   New .... that developed in the nineteenth century reduced the cost of the production of automata.

40   During the nineteenth century, most automata were intended for use by ....

WRITING

WRITING TASK 1

You should spend about 20 minutes on this task.

You work at home and have a problem with a piece of equipment that you use for your job.

Write a letter to the shop or company which supplied the equipment. In your letter

- *describe the problem with the equipment*
- *explain how this problem is affecting your work*
- *say what you want the shop or company to do*

Write at least 150 words.

You do **NOT** need to write any addresses.

Begin your letter as follows:

Dear Sir or Madam,

WRITING TASK 2

You should spend about 40 minutes on this task.

Write about the following topic:

> ***Today more and more tourists are visiting places where conditions are difficult, such as the Sahara desert or the Antarctic.***
>
> ***What are the benefits and disadvantages for tourists who visit such places?***

Give reasons for your answer and include any relevant examples from your own knowledge or experience.

Write at least 250 words.

SPEAKING

PART 1

The examiner asks the candidate about him/herself, his/her home, work or studies and other familiar topics.

EXAMPLE

Health

- Is it important to you to eat healthy food? [Why?/Why not?]
- If you catch a cold, what do you do to help you feel better? [Why?]
- Do you pay attention to public information about health? [Why?/Why not?]
- What could you do to have a healthier lifestyle?

PART 2

Describe an occasion when you had to wait a long time for someone or something to arrive.
 	
You should say:
     who or what you were waiting for
     how long you had to wait
     why you had to wait a long time
and explain how you felt about waiting a long time.

You will have to talk about the topic for one to two minutes.
You have one minute to think about what you are going to say.
You can make some notes to help you if you wish.

PART 3

Discussion topics:

Arriving early

Example questions:
In what kinds of situations should people always arrive early?
How important it is to arrive early in your country?
How can modern technology help people to arrive early?

Being patient

Example questions:
What kinds of jobs require the most patience?
Is it always better to be patient in work (or studies)?
Do you agree or disagree that the older people are, the more patient they are?

Test 6

SECTION 1 Questions 1–10

Complete the notes below.

Write ONE WORD AND/OR A NUMBER for each answer.

Events during Kenton Festival

Example

Start date: ....16th........ May

Opening ceremony (first day)

- In town centre, starting at **1** ....
  The mayor will make a speech
  A **2** .... will perform
  Performance of a **3** .... about Helen Tungate (a **4** ....)
  Evening fireworks display situated across the **5** ....

Other events

- Videos about relationships that children have with their **6** ....
  Venue: **7** .... House

- Performance of **8** .... dances
  Venue: the **9** .... market in the town centre
  Time: 2 and 5 pm every day except 1st day of festival

- Several professional concerts and one by children
  Venue: library
  Time: 6.30 pm on the 18th
  Tickets available online from festival box office and from shops which have
  the festival **10** .... in their windows

---

SECTION 2   *Questions 11–20*

Questions 11–15

*Choose the correct letter, **A**, **B** or **C**.*

Theatre trip to Munich

11 When the group meet at the airport they will have

    A   breakfast.
    B   coffee.
    C   lunch.

12 The group will be met at Munich Airport by

    A   an employee at the National Theatre.
    B   a theatre manager.
    C   a tour operator.

13 How much will they pay per night for a double room at the hotel?

    A   110 euros
    B   120 euros
    C   150 euros

14 What type of restaurant will they go to on Tuesday evening?

    A   an Italian restaurant
    B   a Lebanese restaurant
    C   a typical restaurant of the region

15 Who will they meet on Wednesday afternoon?

    A   an actor
    B   a playwright
    C   a theatre director

Questions 16–20

What does the man say about the play on each of the following days?

*Choose **FIVE** answers from the box and write the correct letter, **A–G**, next to Questions 16–20.*

Comments

A	The playwright will be present.
B	The play was written to celebrate an anniversary.
C	The play will be performed inside a historic building.
D	The play will be accompanied by live music.
E	The play will be performed outdoors.
F	The play will be performed for the first time.
G	The performance will be attended by officials from the town.

Days

16 Wednesday ....

17 Thursday ....

18 Friday ....

19 Saturday ....

20 Monday ....

SECTION 3   *Questions 21–30*

Questions 21–25

Choose the correct letter, A, B or C.

Scandinavian Studies

21   James chose to take Scandinavian Studies because when he was a child

    A   he was often taken to Denmark.
    B   his mother spoke to him in Danish.
    C   a number of Danish people visited his family.

22   When he graduates, James would like to

    A   take a postgraduate course.
    B   work in the media.
    C   become a translator.

23   Which course will end this term?

    A   Swedish cinema
    B   Danish television programmes
    C   Scandinavian literature

24   They agree that James's literature paper this term will be on

    A   19th century playwrights.
    B   the Icelandic sagas.
    C   modern Scandinavian novels.

25   Beth recommends that James's paper should be

    A   a historical overview of the genre.
    B   an in-depth analysis of a single writer.
    C   a study of the social background to the literature.

Questions 26–30

Complete the flow-chart below.

*Choose **FIVE** answers from the box and write the correct letter, **A–G**, next to Questions 26–30.*

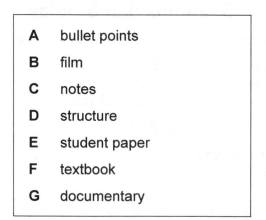

A	bullet points
B	film
C	notes
D	structure
E	student paper
F	textbook
G	documentary

How James will write his paper on the Vikings

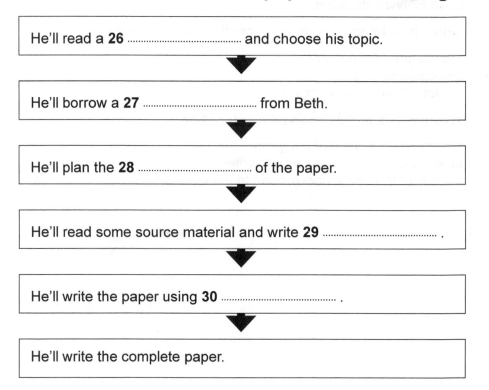

He'll read a **26** .... and choose his topic.

He'll borrow a **27** .... from Beth.

He'll plan the **28** .... of the paper.

He'll read some source material and write **29** ....

He'll write the paper using **30** ....

He'll write the complete paper.

SECTION 4   *Questions 31–40*

Complete the notes below.

*Write **ONE WORD ONLY** for each answer.*

Conflict at work

Conflict mostly consists of behaviour in the general category of **31** ....

Often a result of people wanting to prove their **32** ....

Also caused by differences in **33** .... between people

34 '......................................' conflicts: people more concerned about own team than about company

Conflict-related stress can cause **35** .... that may last for months

Chief Executives (CEOs)

Many have both **36** .... and anxiety

May not like to have their decisions questioned

There may be conflict between people who have different **37** ....

Other managers

A structure that is more **38** .... may create a feeling of uncertainty about who staff should report to.

Minimising conflict

Bosses need to try hard to gain **39** ....

Someone from outside the company may be given the role of **40** .... in order to resolve conflicts.

READING

SECTION 1   *Questions 1–14*

Read the text below and answer Questions 1–7.

Lost, Damaged or Delayed Inland Mail Claim Form

Before completing this claim form for lost, damaged or delayed mail you should visit www.royalmail.com to find out all you need to know about our policies. Alternatively you can get the details from our 'Mail Made Easy' booklet, available at any local post office branch. When you fill in the form, make sure you complete it in full, using the checklist that we have provided to help you. If you find that you do not have the evidence required to make a claim but would like us to investigate an issue with your mail service, the easiest way to do this is by visiting our website.

Lost items

If you wish to claim compensation for lost items, you need to send us original proof of posting, e.g. a Post Office receipt. If claiming for the contents of a package, you also need to provide proof of value, e.g. till item reference number, receipt, bank statement, etc.

Damaged items

When claiming compensation for items that have been damaged, you should send us the items themselves, if possible. However, if these are very large or unsafe to post, you may instead provide photographs as evidence of the damage. Please retain the original packaging (and damaged items, if not sent to us) as we may need to inspect them.

Time restrictions

We allow up to 15 working days for items to arrive, so cannot accept a claim for loss unless 15 working days or more have passed since the item was posted.

Claims for lost or damaged items must be made within 12 months of the postal date. Claims for delayed items must be submitted within 3 months of the date they were posted if the claim is made by the sender, or within 1 month of receipt if the claim is made by the recipient of the item.

Questions 1–7

Complete the notes below.

*Choose **NO MORE THAN TWO WORDS AND/OR A NUMBER** from the text for each answer.*

Write your answers in boxes 1–7 on your answer sheet.

Claiming compensation from the Royal Mail for lost, damaged or delayed mail

Before filling in the form

- go online to learn about their policies or get the **1** .... that contains the relevant information

When filling in the form

- refer to the **2** .... to ensure all the relevant sections are completed

  (You can use their **3** .... to request action if you don't have enough proof to make a claim.)

When claiming compensation for a lost item

- include proof that you have posted the item

- in the case of a package, include something (e.g. bank statement) to prove its **4** ....

When claiming for the cost of a damaged item, include

- either the actual item or **5** .... showing the damage to the item

  (You should keep the **6** .... that was used when the item was originally sent.)

When to claim

- Lost or damaged items: within 12 months of posting the item

- Delayed items: if you are the **7** ...., you must claim within three months of posting the package

Read the text below and answer Questions 8–14.

Days out for the family

A   Carrickfergus Castle

Considered to be Northern Ireland's oldest castle, Carrickfergus has seen more than 800 years of military occupation since its foundations were laid. During summer, traditional feasts are served, and fairs and craft markets provide an extra attraction. The history of the castle is explained and brought to life with exhibits and guided tours.

B   Glamis Castle

Shakespeare used Glamis as the background when he wrote one of his best-known plays, *Macbeth*, and the Queen Mother grew up here. It is also rumoured to have a secret chamber in the walls of the castle. There are many ghost tales associated with this castle, which will capture the imagination of younger visitors.

C   Tintagel Castle

High up on the cliff tops, Tintagel Castle is the legendary home of King Arthur. The visitor's guide on sale at the reception is well worth the money, as it can help you to visualise what it would have been like hundreds of years ago. You can park in the village car park and walk the half mile to the castle, or take the shuttle bus.

D   Pickering Castle

Built by William the Conqueror, this is a great castle for children to run around in. There are lots of special events too, including a chance to come along and see some plays which are put on during the summer months. Nearby Helmsley Castle is also worth a visit.

E   Stokesay Castle

A range of workshops, including music and combat, are held here during the summer. Children of all ages will enjoy learning at these and there is a guided tour which has been especially designed with younger visitors in mind. Some of them may find the dungeon quite scary though.

F   Warwick Castle

This castle is over 1,000 years old and has towers and a moat, and is just as you might imagine a castle to be. Children can even get to try on armour to see how heavy it is. At Christmas, a special market is held here – a great opportunity to look for presents and Christmas treats.

Questions 8–14

*Look at the descriptions of six castles, **A–F**, on page 40.*

For which castle are the following statements true?

*Write the correct letter, **A–F**, in boxes 8–14 on your answer sheet.*

NB *You may use any letter more than once.*

8   At certain times of year you can eat special meals here.

9   Children can get dressed up here.

10   There is another castle in the same area.

11   A lot of stories are told about this place.

12   Part of the castle may be frightening for some children.

13   Plays are performed here during part of the year.

14   A guided tour is offered which is particularly suitable for children.

SECTION 2   *Questions 15–27*

Read the text below and answer Questions 15–20.

North Sydney Council

North Sydney Council recognises the importance of balancing the demands of your work with the demands of your personal life.

The standard working week for full-time council employees is 35 hours for 'Indoor Staff' and 38 hours for 'Outdoor Staff', worked over 5 days. Indoor staff are able to access the benefit of flexi time. A number of these occasionally work from home where appropriate – an example of an initiative that can provide flexibility at certain stages of an employee's career.

Staff are entitled to 3 weeks per annum sick or carer's leave. In addition to the normal parental leave/maternity leave provisions, women who have completed 12 months of continuous service can access a total of 9 weeks' maternity leave that can be taken either as 9 weeks at full pay or as 18 weeks at half pay.

The annual entitlement to paid holidays is 20 days, pro-rata for part-time. After 5 years of continuous service, employees are entitled to 6.5 weeks Long Service Leave (LSL).

Our Financial Advice Program is conducted in partnership with FuturePlus Financial Services. We provide the services of advisors specialising in pensions, and all our employees are given the opportunity to meet them as part of the induction process.

The Employee Assistance Program (EAP) is a counselling service provided at no charge to all employees and their families. The service is available by phone or face to face. The EAP provides registered psychologists for employees wishing to discuss work or non-work matters confidentially. Employees can also access information, such as articles and self assessments, online via eapdirect.

Questions 15–20

Answer the questions below.

Choose **NO MORE THAN TWO WORDS AND/OR A NUMBER** *from the text for each answer.*

Write your answers in boxes 15–20 on your answer sheet.

15 Which employees may choose not to work regular hours?

16 How much time off each year is an employee able to take to look after a relative?

17 What kind of leave involves a choice between two alternative periods of time?

18 How long must employees have worked without a break before being entitled to additional holidays?

19 What does the Financial Advice Program advise staff about?

20 What kind of professional people can employees see if they want to talk about their job in private?

Read the text below and answer Questions 21–27.

Registering As An Apprentice

If you are keen to acquire new skills and learn best through 'hands-on' experiences, then registered apprenticeship is a good option for you. These programmes always involve work experience as well as classroom instruction and produce workers skilled in the occupation. There is a written contract to be signed by the apprentice and the employer, which acknowledges their joint commitment to the training process. This contract is approved and registered by the New York State Department of Labor.

How Do I Qualify?

First of all you must meet the employer's minimum qualifications. This could be a high school diploma or the equivalent. However, some employers will ask for specific high school courses, prior experience, or occupationally related courses.

What Is My Training Like?

Training for each apprenticeable occupation is conducted according to a training outline that has been standardized for the occupation. This assures that apprentices across the state have the same sets of basic competencies and skills. At the successful completion of each registered apprenticeship, the Department of Labor awards the apprentice a 'Certificate of Completion', which is a nationally recognized credential.

The length of time it takes you to learn the skills of the occupation depends upon two things: the standard training outline and your aptitude. Each trade has a definite term of training, listed in years. As a registered apprentice, you may progress according to that established training term, or you may become skilled more quickly or more slowly. It may even be that you start your apprenticeship with credit toward the goal. Your employer may choose to award you this for previous working experience in the occupation, or for prior coursework related to the occupation.

As an apprentice, you are part of the employer's workforce. You work full-time for the employer. A registered apprentice works under the guidance of more experienced craft workers called journey workers. From them, you learn the skills of the trade. As you master each skill, you become a more productive employee.

At the same time as you are working, you are also required to attend classes (usually in the evenings). The location and times of these are set up by the local education agent in consultation with the employer. Your progress is tracked by you, your employer and your education provider.

Successful completion of all requirements results in your certificate.

Questions 21–27

Complete the sentences below.

*Choose **NO MORE THAN TWO WORDS** from the text for each answer.*

Write your answers in boxes 21–27 on your answer sheet.

21 You and your employer will need to sign a .... before training starts.

22 Employers may have different minimum requirements regarding applicants' .... and experience.

23 Each industry has its own standardised .... of training.

24 You may be given credit for work experience or if you have done relevant ....

25 You will be considered as a member of the .... during the apprenticeship.

26 While at work, apprentices are supervised by what are known as ....

27 Employers are consulted when deciding the .... and schedule for lessons.

SECTION 3   *Questions 28–40*

Read the text below and answer Questions 28–34.

Crossing the Humber estuary

A   For thousands of years, the Humber – an estuary formed where two major rivers, the Trent and the Ouse, meet – has been an obstacle to communications along the east coast of England, between the counties of Yorkshire to the north and Lincolnshire to the south. Before the arrival of the railways in the 19th century, water transportation was the most efficient means of moving heavy or bulk freight, and the Humber, situated at the heart of the waterway system associated with the two major rivers, was one of the chief highways of England. Its traffic brought prosperity to the settlements on its banks, particularly the city of Hull on its north bank, but the river itself tended to cut them off from some of their closest neighbours, as well as obstructing the progress of travellers moving north or south.

B   To cater for these local and, as time progressed, wider needs, ferries were provided across many of the streams flowing into the Humber, and in 1315, a ferry was established across the Humber itself between Hull and Lincolnshire. By 1800, this ferry had become fully integrated into the overland transport system, but the changes associated with the industrial revolution were soon to threaten its position. Increased traffic encouraged speculators to establish rival ferries between Hull and Lincolnshire, notably a service between Hull and New Holland which opened in 1826. This crossing was considerably shorter than on the existing Hull to Barton service, which closed in 1851, unable to cope with the increased competition from the rival service.

The New Holland ferry service then grew into a major link between the north and south banks of the Humber, carrying passengers, and cattle and goods bound for Hull Market. In 1968, there was briefly a ferry service from Grimsby to Hull involving hovercrafts. This did not last long as the hovercrafts could not cope with the demands of the River Humber. The ferry service between Hull and New Holland ended with the opening of the Humber Bridge in 1981.

C   The bridge was the outcome of over 100 years of campaigning by local interests for the construction of a bridge or tunnel across the estuary. The first major crossing proposal was a tunnel scheme in 1872. This scheme was promoted by Hull merchants and businesses dissatisfied with the service provided by the New Holland ferry crossing. Over the next 100 years, a variety of proposals were put forward in an effort to bridge the Humber. In 1928, a plan was drawn up by Hull City Council to build a multi-span bridge four miles west of Hull. However, the scheme was dropped after being hit by the financial woes of the Great Depression of the late 1920s and early 1930s.

D   Government approval for the construction of a suspension bridge was finally granted in 1959, although it was not until 1973 that work finally began. The reasons why a suspension bridge was chosen were twofold. Firstly, the Humber has a shifting bed, and the navigable channel along which a craft can travel is always changing; a suspension bridge with no support piers in mid-stream would not obstruct the estuary. Secondly, because of the geology and topography of the area, the cost of constructing a tunnel would have been excessive.

E   Work on the construction proceeded for eight years, during which time many thousands of tonnes of steel and concrete were used and upwards of one thousand workers and staff were employed at times of peak activity. The designers had been responsible for two other major suspension bridges in Britain but, with a total span of 2,220 m, or almost a mile and a half, the Humber was going to be the longest suspension bridge in the world. Nowadays designers have computers, but back then everything was done with slide rules and calculators. The towers were concrete rather than the usual steel, since concrete was cheaper and would blend in better with the setting. The bridge was designed to stand for 120 years.

F   Malcolm Stockwell, the bridgemaster, recalls that when the bridge first opened, there wasn't a great deal of interest in it. Then children started visiting, and he remembers their astonishment at seeing the control room and all the lights. People who lived in towns on opposite banks a mile apart started crossing the river – a journey that previously might as well have been to the moon. The bridge brought them together.

G   The bridge opened up, both socially and economically, two previously remote and insular areas of England, and the improvement in communication enabled the area to realise its potential in commercial, industrial and tourist development. The bridge has saved many millions of vehicle miles and many valuable hours of drivers' and passengers' time – an important factor not only for the drivers and operators of commercial vehicles, but also for tourists and holidaymakers who would have had to travel around the estuary to reach destinations in the region.

In the words of Malcolm Stockwell, 'Although it can't beat the Golden Gate Bridge in San Francisco for setting, it far outstrips it for sheer elegance and as a piece of engineering.'

Questions 28–34

The text on pages 46–47 has seven sections, **A–G**.

Choose the correct heading for each section from the list of headings below.

*Write the correct number, **i–x**, in boxes 28–34 on your answer sheet.*

List of Headings
i   Why the ferry crossing has always been difficult
ii   Building the bridge
iii   An advantage of the design for the bridge
iv   The growing popularity of the bridge
v   Opposition to building a bridge
vi   Benefits and disadvantages the Humber has brought
vii   Proposed alternatives to ferry services
viii   How the bridge has contributed to the region's growth
ix   Rising demand for river transport

28   Section A

29   Section B

30   Section C

31   Section D

32   Section E

33   Section F

34   Section G

Questions 35–40

Complete the summary below.

*Choose **ONE WORD ONLY** from the text for each answer.*

Write your answers in boxes 35–40 on your answer sheet.

Crossing the Humber

The first ferry across the Humber started operating in 1315, and by 1800, this service had been **35** .... with other forms of transport. The mid-19th century saw greater **36** .... in the provision of services. In 1968, an attempt to establish a service across the river using **37** .... failed.

The Humber Bridge is a suspension bridge because the channel that ships travel along moves, and **38** .... supporting a bridge would obstruct it. A bridge rather than a **39** .... was chosen on the grounds of cost. This was also one reason why **40** .... was used for the towers.

WRITING

WRITING TASK 1

You should spend about 20 minutes on this task.

During a recent plane journey, you sat next to a businessman who owns a chain of restaurants. You talked to him and he suggested that you should contact him about a possible job in one of his restaurants.

Write a letter to this businessman. In your letter

- *remind him when and where you met*
- *tell him what kind of job you are interested in*
- *say why you think you would be suitable for the job*

Write at least 150 words.

You do **NOT** need to write any addresses.

Begin your letter as follows:

Dear .... ,

WRITING TASK 2

You should spend about 40 minutes on this task.

Write about the following topic:

> *In many places, new homes are needed, but the only space available for building them is in the countryside. Some people believe it is more important to protect the countryside and not build new homes there.*
>
> *What is your opinion about this?*

Give reasons for your answer and include any relevant examples from your own knowledge or experience.

Write at least 250 words.

SPEAKING

PART 1

The examiner asks the candidate about him/herself, his/her home, work or studies and other familiar topics.

EXAMPLE

Songs and singing

- Did you enjoy singing when you were younger? [Why?/Why not?]
- How often do you sing now? [Why?]
- Do you have a favourite song you like listening to? [Why?/Why not?]
- How important is singing in your culture? [Why?]

PART 2

Describe a film/movie actor from your country who is very popular.
 	
 You should say:
     who this actor is
     what kinds of films/movies he/she acts in
     what you know about this actor's life
 and explain why this actor is so popular.

You will have to talk about the topic for one to two minutes.
You have one minute to think about what you are going to say.
You can make some notes to help you if you wish.

PART 3

Discussion topics:

Watching films/movies

Example questions:
What are the most popular types of films in your country?
What is the difference between watching a film in the cinema and watching a film at home?
Do you think cinemas will close in the future?

Theatre

Example questions:
How important is the theatre in your country's history?
How strong a tradition is it today in your country to go to the theatre?
Do you think the theatre should be run as a business or as a public service?

Test 7

SECTION 1   *Questions 1–10*

Complete the notes below.

*Write **ONE WORD ONLY** for each answer.*

PUBLIC LIBRARY

Example

The library re-opened last .... month ....

The library now has

- a seating area with magazines
- an expanded section for books on **1** ....
- a new section on local **2** ....
- a community room for meetings (also possible to **3** .... there)
- a new section of books for **4** ....

For younger children

- the next Science Club meeting: experiments using things from your **5** ....
- Reading Challenge: read six books during the holidays

For adults

- this Friday: a local author talks about a novel based on a real **6** ....
- IT support is available on Tuesdays – no **7** .... is necessary
- free check of blood **8** .... and cholesterol levels (over 60s only)

Other information

- the library shop sells wall-charts, cards and **9** ....
- evenings and weekends: free **10** .... is available

---

SECTION 2   *Questions 11–20*

Questions 11 and 12

Choose TWO letters, A–E.

Which **TWO** age groups are taking increasing numbers of holidays with BC Travel?

    A   16–30 years
    B   31–42 years
    C   43–54 years
    D   55–64 years
    E   over 65 years

Questions 13 and 14

Choose TWO letters, A–E.

Which **TWO** are the main reasons given for the popularity of activity holidays?

    A   Clients make new friends.
    B   Clients learn a useful skill.
    C   Clients learn about a different culture.
    D   Clients are excited by the risk involved.
    E   Clients find them good value for money.

Questions 15–17

Choose the correct letter, A, B or C.

15   How does BC Travel plan to expand the painting holidays?

    A   by adding to the number of locations
    B   by increasing the range of levels
    C   by employing more teachers

16   Why are BC Travel's cooking holidays unusual?

    A   They only use organic foods.
    B   They have an international focus.
    C   They mainly involve vegetarian dishes.

17   What does the speaker say about the photography holidays?

    A   Clients receive individual tuition.
    B   The tutors are also trained guides.
    C   Advice is given on selling photographs.

Questions 18–20

Complete the table below.

*Write **ONE WORD ONLY** for each answer.*

Fitness Holidays

Location	Main focus	Other comments
Ireland and Italy	general fitness	• personally designed programme • also reduces **18** ....
Greece	**19** .... control	• includes exercise on the beach
Morocco	mountain biking	• wide variety of levels • one holiday that is specially designed for **20** ....

SECTION 3   *Questions 21–30*

Questions 21–26

Complete the flow-chart below.

*Choose **SIX** answers from the box and write the correct letter, **A–H**, next to Questions 21–26.*

A	patterns	**B**	names	**C**	sources	**D**	questions
E	employees	**F**	solutions	**G**	headings	**H**	officials

STAGES IN DOING A TOURISM CASE STUDY

RESEARCH

Locate and read relevant articles, noting key information and also **21** ....
Identify a problem or need

Select interviewees – these may be site **22** .... , visitors or
city **23** ....

Prepare and carry out interviews. If possible, collect statistics.

Check whether **24** .... of interviewees can be used

▼

ANALYSIS

Select relevant information and try to identify **25** ....

Decide on the best form of visuals

▼

WRITING THE CASE STUDY

Give some background before writing the main sections

Do NOT end with **26** ....

Questions 27–30

*Choose the correct letter, **A**, **B** or **C**.*

The Horton Castle site

27 Natalie and Dave agree one reason why so few people visit Horton Castle is that

    A   the publicity is poor.
    B   it is difficult to get to.
    C   there is little there of interest.

28 Natalie and Dave agree that the greatest problem with a visitor centre could be

    A   covering the investment costs.
    B   finding a big enough space for it.
    C   dealing with planning restrictions.

29 What does Dave say about conditions in the town of Horton?

    A   There is a lot of unemployment.
    B   There are few people of working age.
    C   There are opportunities for skilled workers.

30 According to Natalie, one way to prevent damage to the castle site would be to

    A   insist visitors have a guide.
    B   make visitors keep to the paths.
    C   limit visitor numbers.

SECTION 4   *Questions 31–40*

Complete the notes below.

*Write **ONE WORD ONLY** for each answer.*

The effects of environmental change on birds

Mercury (Hg)

- Highly toxic
- Released into the atmosphere from coal
- In water it may be consumed by fish
- It has also recently been found to affect birds which feed on **31** ....

Research on effects of mercury on birds

- Claire Varian-Ramos is investigating:
    - the effects on birds' **32** .... or mental processes, e.g. memory
    - the effects on bird song (usually learned from a bird's **33** ....)
- Findings:
    - songs learned by birds exposed to mercury are less **34** ....
    - this may have a negative effect on birds' **35** ....
- Lab-based studies:
    - allow more **36** .... for the experimenter

Implications for humans

- Migrating birds such as **37** .... containing mercury may be eaten by humans
- Mercury also causes problems in learning **38** ....
- Mercury in a mother's body from **39** .... may affect the unborn child
- New regulations for mercury emissions will affect everyone's energy **40** ....

READING

SECTION 1   *Questions 1–14*

Read the text below and answer Questions 1–7.

Evening Courses

A   Cooking for today

These are classes for those of you who can already make basic meals by keeping strictly to a simple recipe, but who would now like to use your imagination as well. We'll learn how to make great family meals, discovering how to develop basic recipes into personal creations, with a few tricks and tips to help you become more confident.

B   Entertaining the easy way

This course has plenty of ideas and tips for special occasions that you can enjoy preparing, love eating and be proud to provide. The recipes are adaptable to your needs and lifestyle, building on your current skills and aimed at developing your own cooking style.

C   Cooking for the family

Keen to make better food for your kids? This course is for parents who want to learn how to make fun food with the aim of showing their kids how to cook later at home. We'll learn plenty of tasty tips for snacks and picnics, family favourites, and dishes with fresh fruit and vegetables so that you and your family can get really fit and well and enjoy your food.

D   Jewellery making

This course aims to enable students to create silver jewellery. Your first project will be to make a silver ring and then you will have an opportunity to create another piece of your own design. This is an introductory course. Base metals are supplied free. Please wear suitable workshop clothing and bring a notebook and pen.

E   Photography

This course will allow you to take full advantage of your digital camera. Covering portrait, landscape and still-life photography, the classes will include effective use of lenses and lighting. To really benefit from the course, learners should have time to read ahead between sessions.

F   Creative writing

Come and learn how to have fun with stories and other kinds of creative writing. We will try out some new ideas and techniques for improving style and waking up the imagination. Writers who have not taken the foundation class will also be able to join, provided they already have some experience of the subject.

Questions 1–7

*Look at the six advertisements for evening courses, **A–F**, on pages 59–60.*

For which evening course are the following statements true?

*Write the correct letter, **A–F**, in boxes 1–7 on your answer sheet.*

NB *You may use any letter more than once.*

1   After taking this course, participants will be able to teach their skills to others.

2   Participants will be expected to prepare at home for each class.

3   Certain materials will be included in the course fee.

4   This course aims to teach people to prepare meals for guests.

5   This course will help participants to make the best use of a certain item.

6   This course is for people who want to do more than follow instructions.

7   Following this course should improve participants' health.

Read the text on pages 62 and 63 and answer Questions 8–14.

The Bike Foundry

The Bike Foundry aims to promote cycling, and to make an environmentally-friendly means of transport and leisure available to as many people as we can.

Our Bikes

All our bikes are hand-restored by our team and come with a three months' guarantee. We stock bikes to suit different needs, at affordable prices. We gratefully accept donations of unwanted bikes.

Training

We offer maintenance and cycle training to schools and small groups on their own premises. Additionally we provide training to individuals and groups in our workshops.

Maintenance Training

Bike Basics

This is a three-hour course which will teach you everything you need to know to keep on top of simple maintenance issues like looking after brakes and gears and how to repair a puncture. By the end of the course you'll know how to take good care of your bike.

Home Mechanics

This twelve-hour course consists of teaching you how to use specialist tools and how to fit compatible replacement parts. It's aimed at those who have completed Bike Basics or have some prior knowledge.

Courses are run regularly for groups of up to four trainees. We use professional mechanics' tools and employ experienced staff. Most importantly, we have tea- and coffee-making facilities and a fridge where participants can keep their sandwiches, etc. Unfortunately our training room is up a flight of stairs.

For £10 a year you can join our Tool Club. Membership gives you access to our workshop for one evening a week. If you want to repair your bike and know how to fix it, but lack specialist tools, then join our club. There's a range of reference manuals available and a mechanic to offer advice.

Cycling Training

Our qualified instructors can teach you how to ride your bike, whether you have had prior experience or not. If you're already riding and would like to build your confidence, we can teach you safe techniques to negotiate traffic.

Booking Information

To book a place, email training@bikefoundry.org

We ask for a 50% deposit to confirm your place, refundable up to seven days before the course.

Questions 8–14

Do the following statements agree with the information given in the text on pages 62 and 63?

In boxes 8–14 on your answer sheet, write

> **TRUE**   *if the statement agrees with the information*
> **FALSE**   *if the statement contradicts the information*
> **NOT GIVEN** *if there is no information on this*

8   The Bike Foundry sells only second-hand bicycles.

9   All the training sessions are held at the Bike Foundry.

10   The Bike Basics course is aimed at new cyclists.

11   Snacks are provided for participants on the maintenance training courses.

12   Members of the Tool Club have access to cycle reference books.

13   Most of the participants on the Cycling Training courses are beginners.

14   People can cancel their place on a training course one week before it begins and still get their money back.

SECTION 2   *Questions 15–27*

Read the text on pages 65 and 66 and answer Questions 15–21.

Benefits for staff of Hamberton Hospital

Our attractive benefits package is one of the ways we acknowledge the contribution they all make in the provision of high quality patient care. Our package is extensive and varied.

As a Hamberton employee you'll enjoy both National Health Service (NHS) and locally developed schemes, providing you with a range of benefits. These include:

Financial Benefits

- opportunity to contribute to the NHS Pension Scheme – highly regarded by the independent pensions and insurance sector

- Injury Benefits Scheme

- excellent occupational sick pay and maternity leave and pay entitlements

- loans to assist with the purchase of housing for employees in the health service

Work–Life Balance

Here at Hamberton we are committed to helping all employees balance their work and home life commitments. We believe by helping people make this balance we are able to recruit, retain and motivate the most valuable asset of the NHS – our employees. We are committed to making this balance work for all employees equally, not just parents.

Over 50% of our staff work part-time in a range of flexible working options, which include:

- job sharing

- term-time-only working

- part-time working

- individually-tailored working patterns

We also support employees further through our caring and special leave arrangements.

Health

- our own occupational health department, providing a totally confidential service open to all staff during normal working hours

- a round-the-clock free and confidential counselling service

- policies supporting phased returns to work after long illnesses or injuries

Other Benefits

On-site facilities include:

- excellent food provided in our restaurant

- ample parking

- retail outlets

NHS Discounts

All NHS employees can access the NHS Discounts scheme. This allows members of staff free access to a number of discounted products and services. For example, discounts are available at many high street shops and elsewhere, including savings on toys, utility bills, days out, and much more.

Red Guava

This is a further discount benefit, which is available to employees of Hamberton. Red Guava provides discounts on holidays, for example, and can save you money in many other ways too.

Questions 15–21

Complete the sentences below.

*Choose **ONE WORD ONLY** from the text for each answer.*

Write your answers in boxes 15–21 on your answer sheet.

15 The hospital provides benefits to show its recognition of the .... of staff to its work.

16 Financial benefits include pay for staff who are .... or on maternity leave.

17 .... are available for staff who wish to buy a home.

18 Helping staff with their work–life balance is not restricted to ....

19 The hospital has .... that are designed to help staff return to work after a long absence.

20 The facilities on hospital premises include a large area for ....

21 The cost of .... is reduced by using the Red Guava scheme.

Read the text on pages 68 and 69 and answer Questions 22–27.

Performance-related pay

There are a number of reasons why your employer might introduce this type of pay scheme. They may:

- be keen to retain current staff

- want to compete for new talent

- be seeking a fairer way of distributing wages.

In order for performance-related schemes to work they should be based on clear, measurable targets agreed by both employer and employee. You will normally find out about these targets from your contract of employment and the performance appraisal meetings you have with your manager.

Short-term schemes

Short-term schemes usually offer bonus payments, or, depending on the type of work, commission on sales achieved. Payments vary and these schemes are normally used just to encourage staff to improve their own performance.

Long-term schemes

Long-term schemes offer rewards like share options, and can help to encourage loyalty to the organisation and its aims. Such schemes tend to be used as a way of retaining senior staff.

What to do if you have problems

If you don't receive bonus or commission payments which you believe you are owed, check your contract of employment or staff handbook to see how your bonus is paid. Ask your employer if you need more information.

If you think a mistake has been made, you should:

- speak to your employer to see if there has been a misunderstanding

- ask your employer to set out in writing how they have calculated your pay

- keep copies of any letters and notes of any meetings.

There are three ways that the law might cover a case of unpaid bonuses:

- breach of contract
- unlawful deductions from wages
- unlawful discrimination.

Deductions from wages / breach of contract

Any right to a bonus will normally be included in your contract of employment. It may not always be written down. It can be verbally agreed or understood to be there due to normal practice in your particular area of business.

Failure to pay a bonus or commission that you are entitled to could amount to an unlawful deduction of wages.

Discrimination

Your employer must not discriminate against particular groups of people – for example, by giving smaller bonuses to women. Ideally your employer should have some guidelines setting out the normal range of bonuses to give, and these must be followed without discriminating against any specific group.

Questions 22–27

Complete the notes below.

*Choose **ONE WORD ONLY** from the text for each answer.*

Write your answers in boxes 22–27 on your answer sheet.

Performance-related pay

One of the reasons for introducing performance-related pay is in order to **22** .... existing employees

Employer and employee should agree on some **23** .... that can be measured

Short-term schemes: bonus or the payment of a **24** .... related to sales

Long-term reward schemes: generally offered to employees at a **25** .... level

Details of bonus payments: may be included in a contract or a handbook for staff

If you think there has been a mistake with your pay:

• discuss the issue with your employer

• keep records of any relevant **26** ....

It is illegal for employers to discriminate against any specific group, e.g. by giving less money to **27** ....

SECTION 3   *Questions 28–40*

Read the text on pages 72 to 74 and answer Questions 28–40.

Questions 28–34

The text on pages 72 to 74 has seven sections, **A–G**.

Choose the correct heading for each section from the list of headings below.

*Write the correct number, **i–viii**, in boxes 28–34 on your answer sheet.*

List of Headings
i   Plans for more marine protected areas
ii   A historical overview of one specific area
iii Why more has not been done to save marine creatures
iv   What the press has missed
v   Where biodiversity has been shown to help
vi   Who is currently being blamed
vii A reason for some optimism
viii Various factors other than fishing

28   Section **A**

29   Section **B**

30   Section **C**

31   Section **D**

32   Section **E**

33   Section **F**

34   Section **G**

Marine Ecosystems

A

For some time now, the world's oceans and the people who fish them have been a constant source of bad environmental news: cod is effectively an endangered species of fish in some places now; every year thousands of dolphins are injured by fishing vessels; huge tuna farms are ruining the Mediterranean Sea.

What is more, marine biologists recently warned that our seafood is in terminal decline. According to research published in *Science* last November, stocks of all the fish and shellfish that we currently eat will collapse before 2050. Or at least, that's how the media reported it.

B

However, the scientist who led the study has said that the main conclusion of his research has been buried beneath the headlines. While the danger to our seafood supply is real enough, says Boris Worm, assistant professor of marine conservation biology at Dalhousie University, Canada, there is a more serious point: that the way in which we manage the oceans is not only threatening the survival of individual species, it's upsetting the delicate balance of marine communities and thus causing the collapse of entire ecosystems. Research has shown that the number of ecosystems where all higher forms of life are extinct, so-called dead zones, is increasing.

The point that many reports failed to highlight, says Worm, is that we have to revolutionise the way our marine resources are run, changing the focus from stocks and quotas to biodiversity and ecosystem protection. And to do that, we must change the way the debate about our marine resources is conducted in the public domain.

C

Around 7,500 years ago, shrinking glaciers and the resulting higher water levels led to the development of what's called the Wadden Sea, a 13,500-square-kilometre area of the North Sea. During the first 5,000 years or so, the sea pulsated with life. There was a high level of biodiversity on the seabed too, and the salt marshes and mud flats on the coast supported millions of birds. This continued until around 2,000 years ago, when human pressure began to affect it. Research has shown that some of the larger creatures disappeared more than 500 years ago. And by the late 19th century, populations of most of the other mammals and fish were severely reduced, leading to the collapse of several traditional fisheries.

D

What's interesting is that overfishing isn't the main agent of the decline, as we might assume. It's due to an ongoing combination of exploitation, habitat destruction and pollution. Coastal development, for example, destroys large areas of wetlands that support a range of species. Pollution fuels a process known as eutrophication, which kills certain seagrasses. Nutrients such as nitrogen and phosphorus contained in human and industrial waste promote the growth of tiny phytoplankton. This over-enrichment of the sea can ultimately lead to the collapse of the entire system through oxygen starvation.

Most marine ecosystems have an in-built capacity to deal with a certain amount of pollution because shellfish can absorb phytoplankton. But in many cases, these have been largely removed by fishing, so the effect of any nutrient-rich pollutants entering the system is increased. In a healthy system, coastal wetlands also act as filters, so their destruction causes even more pollution. These processes have been fairly well understood for a number of years.

E

What the *Science* paper has demonstrated, however, is that the decline in the health of ecosystems is greater where the number of different species is low. The population of marbled rock cod around the South Atlantic island of South Georgia, for example, still hasn't recovered after the fishing industry caused its collapse during the 1970s. By contrast, North Sea cod has withstood very heavy fishing for hundreds of years, says Worm, and although it has declined substantially, it hasn't yet collapsed completely. Worm believes that, 'to have a greater number of species makes an ecosystem more robust'. His theory is backed up by evidence from experiments into how ecosystems react to change.

F

And some positive news came from the study. Worm and his colleagues were able to show that it's possible to reverse such damage as long as there are enough species. A survey of 44 protected areas revealed increases in biodiversity and fish catches close to the reserves. Worm says, 'We should be focusing our attention on protecting all of our marine resources at the ecosystem level, and managing levels of fishing, pollution and habitat disturbance to ensure that crucial services that maintain the health of the ecosystem continue to function.' To anyone who knows anything about ecology, it would appear that Worm is just stating the obvious. And many protected areas on land are now managed in this way.

G

However, there has long been a tendency to view our oceans as a limitless resource, combined with a widespread failure to make an emotional connection with most marine wildlife. True, we have created a small number of marine protected areas. 'We seem to have understood the value of protecting ecosystems in areas such as the Australian Great Barrier Reef that we consider to be particularly beautiful,' says John Shepherd, Professor of Marine Sciences at Southampton University in the UK. 'Human nature will always draw us towards those species or habitats that are more aesthetically pleasing. That's why there will always be support for protecting pandas and very little for worms, even though nematodes play a vital role in maintaining the health of an ecosystem.'

Questions 35–37

*Choose the correct letter, **A**, **B**, **C** or **D**.*

Write the correct letter in boxes 35–37 on your answer sheet.

35 Boris Worm's main concern is that

    A marine ecosystems will completely break down.
    B insufficient attention is being paid to fish numbers.
    C there will no longer be enough seafood for people to eat.
    D politicians will be unwilling to discuss marine resources.

36 What point does John Shepherd make?

    A Marine conservation areas are not high on the list of visitor attractions.
    B People know very little about how different species actually live.
    C The public are much less likely to help unattractive creatures.
    D The marine environment was better understood in the past.

37 Which of the following best summarises the text as a whole?

    A Scientists disagree about the state of the world's oceans.
    B A radical review of marine resource management is needed.
    C The fishing industry is mainly responsible for today's problems.
    D The natural systems of our seas will not be able to repair themselves.

Questions 38–40

Complete the summary below.

*Choose **ONE WORD ONLY** from the text for each answer.*

Write your answers in boxes 38–40 on your answer sheet.

The Wadden Sea

The Wadden Sea was created when the sea rose as a consequence of **38** .... slowly contracting. The waters were full of different species of marine creatures, and there were large numbers of **39** .... living on the wetlands along the shore. This continued until species began to decline 2,000 years ago. Overfishing was partly responsible for the changing circumstances, and so was pollution. At the same time there has been an increase in some nutrients in the Wadden Sea which can also destroy marine creatures and vegetation by depriving them of **40** .... which is essential for their survival.

WRITING

WRITING TASK 1

You should spend about 20 minutes on this task.

> *A large company in your area has decided to spend a certain amount of money, either to sponsor a local children's sports team for two years, or to pay for two open-air concerts. It has asked for feedback from the general public.*
>
> *Write a letter to the company. In your letter*
> - *describe the benefits of sponsoring the sports team*
> - *summarise the benefits of paying for the concerts*
> - *say how you think the company should spend the money*

Write at least 150 words.

You do **NOT** need to write any addresses.

Begin your letter as follows:

Dear Sir or Madam,

WRITING TASK 2

You should spend about 40 minutes on this task.

Write about the following topic:

> **Some people say that parents should encourage their children to take part in organised group activities in their free time. Others say that it is important for children to learn how to occupy themselves on their own.**
>
> **Discuss both these views and give your own opinion.**

Give reasons for your answer and include any relevant examples from your own knowledge or experience.

Write at least 250 words.

SPEAKING

PART 1

The examiner asks the candidate about him/herself, his/her home, work or studies and other familiar topics.

EXAMPLE

Clothes

- Where do you buy most of your clothes? [Why?]
- How often do you buy new clothes for yourself? [Why?]
- How do you decide which clothes to buy? [Why?]
- Have the kinds of clothes you like changed in recent years? [Why?/Why not?]

PART 2

Describe an interesting discussion you had about how you spend your money.
 	
You should say:
    who you had the discussion with
    why you discussed this topic
    what the result of the discussion was
and explain why this discussion was interesting for you.

You will have to talk about the topic for one to two minutes. You have one minute to think about what you are going to say. You can make some notes to help you if you wish.

PART 3

Discussion topics:

Money and young people

Example questions:
Why do some parents give their children money to spend each week?
Do you agree that schools should teach children how to manage money?
Do you think it is a good idea for students to earn money while studying?

Money and society

Example questions:
Do you think it is true that in today's society money cannot buy happiness?
What disadvantages are there in a society where the gap between rich and poor is very large?
Do you think richer countries have a responsibility to help poorer countries?

Test 8

SECTION 1   Questions 1–10

Complete the notes below.

*Write **ONE WORD AND/OR A NUMBER** for each answer.*

Cycle tour leader: Applicant enquiry

Example

Name: Margaret .... Smith ....

About the applicant:

- wants a **1** .... job
- will soon start work as a **2** ....
- has led cycle trips in **3** ....
- interested in being a leader of a cycling trip for families
- is currently doing voluntary work with members of a **4** .... club
- available for five months from the 1st of **5** ....
- can't eat **6** ....

Contact details:

- address: 27 **7** .... Place, Dumfries
- postcode: **8** ....

Interview:

- interview at 2.30 pm on **9** ....
- will plan a short **10** .... about being a tour guide

SECTION 2   *Questions 11–20*

Questions 11–14

*Choose the correct letter, **A**, **B** or **C**.*

Visiting the Sheepmarket area

11 Which is the most rapidly-growing group of residents in the Sheepmarket area?

    A   young professional people
    B   students from the university
    C   employees in the local market

12 The speaker recommends the side streets in the Sheepmarket for their

    A   international restaurants.
    B   historical buildings.
    C   arts and crafts.

13 Clothes designed by entrants for the Young Fashion competition must

    A   be modelled by the designers themselves.
    B   be inspired by aspects of contemporary culture.
    C   be made from locally produced materials.

14 Car parking is free in some car parks if you

    A   stay for less than an hour.
    B   buy something in the shops.
    C   park in the evenings or at weekends.

Questions 15–20

Label the map below.

*Write the correct letter, **A–I**, next to Questions 15–20.*

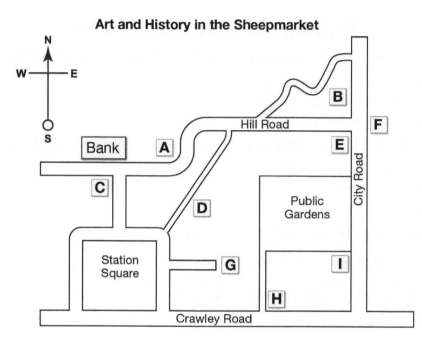

Art and History in the Sheepmarket

15	The Reynolds House	....
16	The Thumb	....
17	The Museum	....
18	The Contemporary Art Gallery	....
19	The Warner Gallery	....
20	Nucleus	....

SECTION 3   *Questions 21–30*

Questions 21–24

Complete the table below.

*Write **ONE WORD ONLY** for each answer.*

Presentation on film adaptations of Shakespeare's plays

Stages of presentation	Work still to be done
Introduce Giannetti's book containing a **21** .... of adaptations	Organise notes
Ask class to suggest the **22** .... adaptations	No further work needed
Present Rachel Malchow's ideas	Prepare some **23** ....
Discuss relationship between adaptations and **24** .... at the time of making the film	No further work needed

Questions 25–30

What do the speakers say about each of the following films?

*Choose **SIX** answers from the box and write the correct letter, **A–G**, next to questions 25–30.*

Comments
A clearly shows the historical period
B contains only parts of the play
C is too similar to another kind of film
D turned out to be unpopular with audiences
E presents the play in a different period from the original
F sets the original in a different country
G incorporates a variety of art forms

Films

25 *Ran*   ....

26 *Much Ado About Nothing*   ....

27 *Romeo & Juliet*   ....

28 *Hamlet*   ....

29 *Prospero's Books*   ....

30 *Looking for Richard*   ....

SECTION 4   *Questions 31–40*

Complete the notes below.

*Write **ONE WORD ONLY** for each answer.*

Noise in Cities

Past research focused on noise level (measured in decibels) and people's responses.

Noise 'maps'

- show that the highest noise levels are usually found on roads
- do not show other sources of noise, e.g. when windows are open or people's neighbours are in their **31** ....
- ignore variations in people's perceptions of noise
- have made people realize that the noise is a **32** .... issue that must be dealt with

Problems caused by noise

- sleep disturbance
- increase in amount of stress
- effect on the **33** .... of schoolchildren

Different types of noise

Some noises can be considered pleasant e.g. the sound of a **34** .... in a town

To investigate this, researchers may use methods from **35** .... sciences e.g. questionnaires

What people want

Plenty of activity in urban environments which are **36** .... , but also allow people to relax

But architects and town planners

- do not get much **37** .... in acoustics
- regard sound as the responsibility of engineers

Understanding sound as an art form

We need to know

- how sound relates to **38** ....
- what can be learnt from psychology about the effects of sound
- whether physics can help us understand the **39** .... of sound

Virtual reality programs

- advantage: predict the effect of buildings
- current disadvantage: they are **40** ....

READING

SECTION 1   *Questions 1–14*

Read the text below and answer Questions 1–6.

Music Clubs

A   Whitehay Youth Music is intended for anyone aged between 6 and 14 who is keen to perform in public. The club is limited to 30 members at any time, and we operate a waiting list for membership. Two concerts are performed every year, and every member takes part. Members must have reached at least an intermediate standard on their instrument. The group meets in the Jubilee Hall on Wednesday evenings during term time for rehearsals and for workshops in which members learn how to improve their playing.

B   Whitehay Music Club brings together music lovers from around the district, for enjoyable evenings of food and music. We meet monthly in members' homes, and during the evening we have a buffet meal and listen to recordings of both well-known and not so well-known music. The music is preceded by a brief talk providing background information about the composers and the music. Every few months we organise a coach trip to a musical event within a radius of 50 km.

C   Whitehay Philharmonic is an amateur orchestra, founded in 1954. Two or three times a year, it performs a wide range of music to large and appreciative audiences from the area, in the town's Jubilee Hall. New members are always welcome, and can take part in rehearsals, although there may not be room for everyone to perform in the concerts. Because the orchestra only partly finances its performances through ticket sales, members with marketing experience are particularly welcome, in order to build sales.

D   Whitehay Music Society is primarily a fundraising group that organises a range of money-making activities – from street collections to seeking sponsorship from local businesses. The money raised is used to support professional musicians if, for example, illness prevents them from earning a living. As a member, you will receive a monthly newsletter describing our work, and containing details of concerts, operas and other performances, both locally and nationally. Everybody is welcome to join the society: children are particularly welcome, along with their parents.

Questions 1–8

*Look at the four advertisements for music clubs in a town called Whitehay, **A–D**, on page 86.*

For which club are the following statements true?

*Write the correct letter, **A–D**, in boxes 1–8 on your answer sheet.*

1   It needs members who can find ways of increasing audience numbers.

2   All its members perform in club concerts.

3   It distributes information about musical events to its members.

4   It requires its members to have reached a certain level as performers.

5   One of its aims is to introduce its members to music they may not be familiar with.

6   It helps children to develop their musical skills.

7   Its performances are popular with local people.

8   It helps people who are in financial need.

Read the text below and answer Questions 9–14.

Biological Research Institute

Welcome to the Biological Research Institute campus. We hope that your visit will be enjoyable and interesting. Please read the information below and comply with the instructions given.

On arrival, you should report to the Reception building by the main entrance gate, where you will be issued with a pass. This must be visible at all times during your visit to the campus.

If you are driving a vehicle, please inform Reception. They will contact Security, who will identify the area where you should park your car. Please ensure that you park it in the designated area. You must keep to the campus speed limit (10 mph) at all times. Cars are parked at the owner's risk.

For your own safety, please follow the instructions displayed on noticeboards around the campus, as well as all instructions issued by authorised personnel. Do not enter any restricted areas or touch any machinery or other equipment unless authorised. Visitors must be accompanied by their host at all times whilst on the campus.

Entry into certain areas requires the wearing of special clothing or equipment. This will be provided for you by your host, who will advise you on the appropriate protection for the areas you visit.

Unless your host has previously obtained permission from the Institute management, photography, whether still or video, is not permitted in any part of the campus.

Children under the age of 16 must be accompanied by an adult at all times, and should only be brought on campus if the Institute management has previously agreed to this. No nursery facilities are available for visiting children.

In the event of an accident, call 3333 and request the assistance of site first-aid personnel.

Questions 9–14

Complete the sentences below.

Choose **ONE WORD ONLY** *from the text for each answer.*

Write your answers in boxes 9–14 on your answer sheet.

9   If you come by car, ... will tell you where to park it.

10   Advice on .... can be seen on noticeboards.

11   You will need to obtain authorisation before touching equipment such
     as ....

12   Permission from the management is required if you want to do any kind
     of ....

13   The Institute does not provide a .... for children visiting the campus.

14   You should phone 3333 if any kind of .... occurs.

SECTION 2   *Questions 15–27*

Read the text below and answer Questions 15–20.

Negotiating a better salary package for your new job

If you make it through the recruitment interview, a job offer may be just around the corner and you face having to talk about the nitty-gritty: your financial value.

Although many graduate training schemes have set starting salaries, there are loads of other jobs where you'll need to exercise your negotiating skills. If you're offered a job, it's because the organisation sees you as a valuable asset and you should try to set your level of remuneration accordingly.

There are no general rules about how and when to conduct your negotiation but being sensitive to the culture of the organisation is essential. There are also some practical steps you can take to position yourself sensibly. Familiarise yourself with the company itself, as well as the range of salaries on offer. Doing careful research in this way prior to starting negotiations is very valuable. You can look at the range of packages offered for comparable jobs in adverts on the internet, or ask for advice from people you know professionally or personally. You could also approach a local Training and Enterprise Council. Finally, if you're a member of a union, they will have information on acceptable salary ranges for your profession.

If the salary offered is less than you'd hoped for, you could negotiate an early pay review instead, say after the first six months. Ensure that the criteria are clearly set out though, and that they're included in your contract.

Make sure you check out the salary package, not just the number of zeroes on your payslip. You may find that the total package of pay and benefits raises the worth of the salary to an acceptable level. For instance, you may be offered private health cover, a non-contributory pension, a car to use for work purposes and/or significant bonuses. When bonuses are mentioned, you may want to discuss the basis on which they're paid, so that you're absolutely clear about the terms and conditions attached. When negotiating, be persuasive and consistent in your arguments but be prepared to agree to a compromise if you really want the job.

If your negotiations are successful, ask for the agreed terms and conditions to be confirmed in writing ASAP.

Questions 15–20

Complete the sentences below.

*Choose **ONE WORD ONLY** from the text for each answer.*

Write your answers in boxes 15–20 on your answer sheet.

15 When negotiating a salary, potential employees should take advantage of the company's view of them as a useful ....

16 When negotiating a salary it is important to be aware of the company's particular ....

17 Some people use the .... to monitor salaries offered for similar positions.

18 People who belong to a .... can ask for recommendations on what is the norm for payment in their field.

19 Some people try to arrange for a .... of their salary to be carried out after an initial period.

20 It is important to be willing to accept a .... if the negotiations are getting nowhere.

Read the text on pages 92 and 93 and answer Questions 21–27.

How to run a successful project

A project manager's main task is to bring a particular project to completion, both on time and within budget. There are many factors that can cause a project to veer off its tracks, but steps can be taken to ensure that your project experiences as little disruption as possible.

1. Prepare the framework

If you get everything down in writing at the beginning of the project, you have an excellent foundation to build upon. Change is inevitable, but you have to maintain control. This is critical to avoid problems of 'scope creep', which is when the company paying for the project asks for 'just one more little thing' repeatedly, until the project becomes unmanageable.

2. Select the team

Gather your human resources, and make sure that their skills align with their roles. This is an important first step: if you assign the wrong person to a task, you are reducing your chances of success.

Make sure each team member is clear on what is expected from them and when. Encourage them to ask questions to clarify anything that may be uncertain, and to always come to you whenever something seems to be out of place or going wrong. Clear communication is critical.

Make sure the whole team and the client company grasp the project's limitations in terms of its achievable outcomes. You can finish a task successfully and on time as long as expectations are reasonable.

3. Staying on track

How can you know if your project is going to be successful if you don't have any way of measuring success? You will need interim milestones, especially for a long-term project, so that you can determine if you are staying on track or straying from the project's goals.

4. Manage project risks

Hopefully you have defined the more likely risks up front during the project preparation, so you should now put contingency plans in place for certain occurrences. If you can see when a risk is imminent, you can take preventive action to avoid it, but be ready to halt a project if the risk becomes unacceptable.

5. Evaluate the project

Once a project has been completed, it's important to write a report, even if it is only for internal purposes. You can pinpoint what went right or wrong, determine what could have been done differently, and establish the best practices for use in future undertakings.

Questions 21–27

Complete the flow-chart below.

*Choose **NO MORE THAN TWO WORDS** from the text for each answer.*

Write your answers in boxes 21–27 on your answer sheet.

How to run a successful project

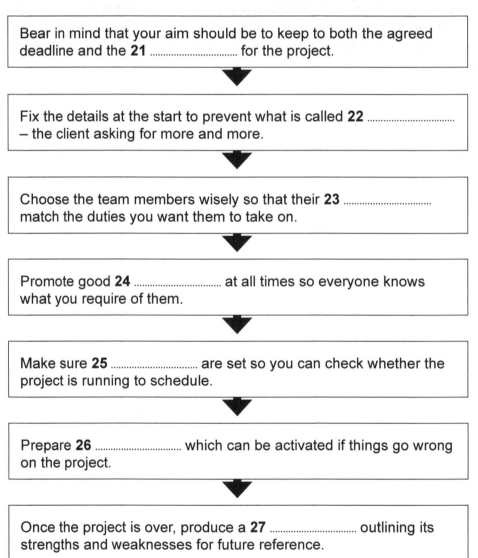

Bear in mind that your aim should be to keep to both the agreed deadline and the **21** .... for the project.

Fix the details at the start to prevent what is called **22** ....
– the client asking for more and more.

Choose the team members wisely so that their **23** ....
match the duties you want them to take on.

Promote good **24** .... at all times so everyone knows what you require of them.

Make sure **25** .... are set so you can check whether the project is running to schedule.

Prepare **26** .... which can be activated if things go wrong on the project.

Once the project is over, produce a **27** .... outlining its strengths and weaknesses for future reference.

SECTION 3   *Questions 28–40*

Read the text on pages 95 and 96 and answer Questions 28–40.

Mass appeal of the manta rays

A   I am underwater, face to face with a large flat fish which I recognise immediately as being a manta ray. For an instant I look straight into its gaping mouth and see the row of small, flattened teeth in its lower jaw. Close on its tail comes another manta ray, and another and another. The manta rays are unaffected by my being there, cruising past in a leisurely fashion without seeming to expend any great effort.

B   From above, the manta rays are great black silhouettes that fishermen called 'devil fish', because of the curious horn-like fins hanging down near their mouths. But looking into their eyes you get a sense of their peaceful nature. Unlike stingrays, mantas don't have venomous spines in their tails, and unlike many fish species they seem to enjoy human company. Once, over-enthusiastically, I swim towards a manta. I am just a few inches away when it senses me. To my surprise, the whole fish twitches in alarm and shoots off, perhaps fearing that I will touch it. I feel ashamed to have given it a fright.

C   I have come to Hanifaru, a small lagoon next to an uninhabited island in the Maldives, especially to see manta rays. These great harmless creatures congregate here during the south-west monsoons between May and November and, if the tides and winds are right, enter a shallow cul-de-sac in the reef to hunt for plankton, their main source of nutrition. On certain days the bay can attract more than 100 mantas. I have seen many manta rays on dives around the world, though not in these numbers.

D   Guy Stevens is my guide, a British marine biologist who has been studying the mantas for the past five years. Based at the nearby Four Seasons resort, he has identified more than 2,000 individual manta rays, photographing and cataloguing them according to their distinctive skin patterns. Each day we make the 40-minute boat journey from the resort to Hanifaru. Feeding events, as Guy calls them, are never guaranteed, but, during the season, hotel guests can sign up for 'manta alerts'. If Guy and his research assistants spot significant manta activity, the guests will be brought by fast speedboat to the lagoon to snorkel. When feeding, the mantas of Hanifaru tend to stay near the surface, making them accessible to snorkellers just as much as divers. They seem not to mind the human competition in this quite small space, and indeed they are often joined by other rays and even giant whale sharks, which feed on the same plankton.

E Word among the diving community about the possibility of finding a mass of manta rays at Hanifaru has slowly been spreading over the past year. Outside the shallow lagoon I can see five large safari boats – live-aboard cruisers that take divers around the best underwater sites in the Maldives. It is something that Guy has been monitoring closely. 'Word is out that Hanifaru is a top manta spot,' he explains, 'and although the government has declared the bay a "protected area", we still don't have any regulations in force to limit the number of people in the water at any one time.'

F During my stay, the resort received a visit from the then-president of the Maldives, Mohamed Nasheed. Since coming to power in 2008, he had made his interest in the marine environment and concerns about climate change well known. In 2009 he held an underwater cabinet meeting, urging other world leaders to act decisively to combat climate change. The protection of wildlife areas such as Hanifaru was clearly one of his objectives, and I asked him why he took such an interest. 'Maldivians have lived with the reefs and their fish life since long before there were tourists,' he said. 'And while tourist dollars are good for our country, the sea and its produce are even more vital to my people. I have to balance what tourists want to see with preserving the marine environment – and in some cases, like Hanifaru, those objectives coincide.'

G On several dives I am lucky enough to get close to the mantas, sometimes at underwater 'cleaning stations'. Here, the mantas come in small numbers, or individually, to pause above a coral outcrop and wait while small fish pick at their skin, removing parasites. Adapted for fast swimming with their flattened bodies, they can accelerate rapidly with a twitch of their wings. They gaze at human swimmers with a kind of knowing calm, something people often remark on when they try to capture the emotion they experience after seeing them. 'The manta rays have the biggest brain of any fish,' Guy explains, 'and some manta researchers are convinced that mantas can recognise individual people underwater.'

H I return to the lagoon over the course of several days and learn more from Guy about his hopes for the future. 'People can visit this place, but I want to be sure that they don't harass the mantas by touching them or crowding them out while they're feeding. We're working to get a full-time ranger station and some kind of permit system to limit the number of boats that can enter the lagoon each day.'

Questions 28–30

*The text on pages 95 and 96 has 8 paragraphs, **A–H**.*

Which paragraph mentions the following?

*Write the correct letter, **A–H**, in boxes 28–30 on your answer sheet.*

28   a record that is being kept of manta rays in the area

29   something that the writer regrets

30   the reason for the writer's visit

Questions 31–36

Do the following statements agree with the information given in the text on pages 95 and 96?

In boxes 31–36 on your answer sheet, write

> **TRUE**   *if the statement agrees with the information*
> **FALSE**   *if the statement contradicts the information*
> **NOT GIVEN** *if there is no information on this*

31   It is difficult to distinguish one manta ray from another.

32   For hotel guests, viewing manta rays feeding has to be arranged at short notice.

33   The manta rays appear to object to the presence of people in the water while they are feeding.

34   Guy Stevens is concerned about the increasing interest in Hanifaru.

35   Mohamed Nasheed succeeded in persuading certain other countries to take steps to protect the environment.

36   A procedure has now been established to control the number of visitors.

Questions 37–40

Complete the summary below.

Choose **ONE WORD ONLY** from the text for each answer.

Write your answers in boxes 37–40 on your answer sheet.

The manta ray

During certain times of year, depending on the weather conditions and the tides, manta rays collect to look for **37** .... to feed on. They eat the same food as other species, such as giant whale sharks. As for keeping clean, they are kept free from **38** .... by smaller fish.

Manta rays have certain characteristics which make them good swimmers; they use their **39** .... to get up speed and they have flattened bodies, which help them to move quickly through the water. The nature of the manta's **40** .... is of particular interest to scientists.

WRITING

WRITING TASK 1

You should spend about 20 minutes on this task.

There have been several complaints about the reception area where visitors to your company arrive. Your manager has asked you to suggest how the reception area could be improved.

Write a letter to your manager. In your letter
- **describe the complaints that have been made**
- **say why the reception area is important**
- **suggest how the reception area could be improved**

Write at least 150 words.

You do **NOT** need to write any addresses.

Begin your letter as follows:

Dear .... ,

WRITING TASK 2

You should spend about 40 minutes on this task.

Write about the following topic:

> **In recent years, many small local shops have closed because customers travel to large shopping centres or malls to do their shopping.**
>
> **Is this a positive or a negative development?**

Give reasons for your answer and include any relevant examples from your own knowledge or experience.

Write at least 250 words.

SPEAKING

PART 1

The examiner asks the candidate about him/herself, his/her home, work or studies and other familiar topics.

EXAMPLE

Art

- Did you enjoy doing art lessons when you were a child? [Why?/Why not?]
- Do you ever draw or paint pictures now? [Why?/Why not?]
- When was the last time you went to an art gallery or exhibition? [Why?]
- What kind of pictures do you like having in your home? [Why?]

PART 2

Describe a time when you visited a friend or family member at their workplace.

You should say:
 who you visited
 where this person worked
 why you visited this person's workplace
and explain how you felt about visiting this person's workplace.

You will have to talk about the topic for one to two minutes. You have one minute to think about what you are going to say. You can make some notes to help you if you wish.

PART 3

Discussion topics:

Different kinds of workplaces

Example questions:
What things make an office comfortable to work in?
Why do some people prefer to work outdoors?
Do you agree that the building people work in is more important than the colleagues they work with?

The importance of work

Example questions:
What would life be like if people didn't have to work?
Are all jobs of equal importance?
Why do some people become workaholics?

Audioscripts

TEST 5

SECTION 1

TC EMPLOYEE:	Hi. Can I help you?
VISITOR:	I'd like to find out if you have any excursions suitable for families.
TC EMPLOYEE:	Sure. How about taking your family for a cruise? <u>We have a steamship that takes passengers out several times a day</u> – it's over 100 years old.

Example

VISITOR:	That sounds interesting. How long is the trip?
TC EMPLOYEE:	About an hour and a half. <u>And don't forget to take pictures of the mountains.</u> They're all around you when you're on the boat and they look fantastic.

Q1

VISITOR:	OK. And I assume there's a café or something on board?
TC EMPLOYEE:	Sure. How old are your children?
VISITOR:	Er, my daughter's fifteen and my son's seven.
TC EMPLOYEE:	Right. Well there are various things you can do once you've crossed the lake, to make a day of it. One thing that's very popular is a visit to the Country Farm. You're met off the boat by the farmer and he'll take you to the holding pens, where the sheep are kept. Children love feeding them!
VISITOR:	My son would love that. He really likes animals.
TC EMPLOYEE:	Well, <u>there's also a 40-minute trek round the farm on a horse</u>, if he wants.

Q2

VISITOR:	Do you think he'd manage it? He hasn't done that before.
TC EMPLOYEE:	Sure. It's suitable for complete beginners.
VISITOR:	Ah, good.
TC EMPLOYEE:	And again, visitors are welcome to explore the farm on their own, as long as they take care to close gates and so on. <u>There are some very beautiful gardens along the side of the lake which also belong to the farm</u> – they'll be just at their best now. You could easily spend an hour or two there.

Q3

VISITOR:	OK. Well that all sounds good. <u>And can we get lunch there</u>?

Q4

TC EMPLOYEE:	<u>You can, and it's very good, though it's not included in the basic cost. You pay when you get there.</u>
VISITOR:	Right.

VISITOR:	So is there anything else to do over on that side of the lake?
TC EMPLOYEE:	Well, what you can do is take a bike over on the ship and then go on a cycling trip. There's a trail there called the Back Road – you could easily spend three or four hours exploring it, and the scenery's wonderful. <u>They'll give you a map when you get your ticket for the cruise – there's no extra charge.</u>

Q5

VISITOR:	What's the trail like in terms of difficulty?
TC EMPLOYEE:	Quite challenging in places. It wouldn't be suitable for your seven-year-old. <u>It needs someone who's got a bit more experience.</u>

Q6

VISITOR:	Hmm. Well, my daughter loves cycling and so do I, so maybe the two of us could go, and my wife and son could stay on the farm. That might work out quite well. But we don't have bikes here... is there somewhere we could rent them?
TC EMPLOYEE:	Yes, there's a place here in the city. <u>It's called Ratchesons.</u>

Q7

VISITOR:	I'll just make a note of that – er, how do you spell it?

TC EMPLOYEE:	R-A-T-C-H-E-S-O-N-S. It's just by the cruise ship terminal.
VISITOR:	OK.
TC EMPLOYEE:	You'd also need to pick up a repair kit for the bike from there to take along with you, and you'd need to take along a snack and some water – it'd be best to get those in the city.
VISITOR:	Fine. That shouldn't be a problem. <u>And I assume I can rent a helmet from the bike place?</u> *Q8*
TC EMPLOYEE:	<u>Sure, you should definitely get that</u>. It's a great ride, but you want to be well prepared because <u>it's very remote – you won't see any shops round there, or anywhere to stay</u>, so you need to get back in time for the last boat. *Q9*
VISITOR:	Yeah. So what sort of prices are we looking at here?
TC EMPLOYEE:	Let's see, that'd be one adult and one child for the cruise with farm tour, that's $117, and an adult and a child for the cruise only so that's $214 dollars altogether. Oh, wait a minute, how old did you say your daughter was?
VISITOR:	Fifteen.
TC EMPLOYEE:	Then I'm afraid <u>it's $267</u> because she has to pay the adult fare, which is $75 instead of the child fare which is $22 – sorry about that. *Q10*
VISITOR:	That's OK. Er, so how do ...

SECTION 2

Good morning everyone. My name's Joy Parkins and I'm the restaurant manager. And I understand that none of you've had any previous experience as kitchen assistants? Well, you might be feeling a bit nervous now, but most of our kitchen assistants say they enjoy the work. OK, they might get shouted at sometimes, but it's nothing personal, and <u>they're pleased that they have so many different things to do, which means they never get bored</u>. And I'll *Q11* tell you straightaway that if you do well, we might think about moving you up and giving you some more responsibility.

Right, well, you've all shown up on time, which is an excellent start. Now I'm glad to see none of you have unsuitable footwear, so that's good – you need to be careful as the floors can get very wet and slippery. Those of you with long hair have got it well out of the way, <u>but some of you'll need to remove your rings and bracelets – just put them somewhere safe for today, and remember to leave them at home tomorrow, as they can be a safety hazard</u>. *Q12*

<u>Now it's going to be a busy day for you all today – we don't have any tables free for this evening, and only a few for lunch.</u> Fortunately we've got our Head Chef back – he was away *Q13* on holiday all last week which meant the other chefs had extra work. Now, I'll tell you a bit more about the job in a minute but first, some general regulations. For all of you, whatever your age, there's some equipment you mustn't use until you've been properly trained, like the waste disposal system for example, for health and safety reasons. <u>Then I think there are two of you here who are under 18 – that's Emma and Jake, isn't it? Right, so for you two, the meat slicer is out of bounds.</u> And of course none of you are allowed to use the electric mixer *Q14* until you've been shown how it works.

Now you may have heard that this can be a stressful job, and I have to say that can be true. You'll be working an eight-hour day for the first week, though you'll have the chance to do overtime after that as well if you want to. But however long the hours are, you'll get a break in the middle. <u>What you will find is that you're on your feet all day long, lifting and carrying, so</u> *Q15 &* <u>if you're not fit now you soon will be! You'll find you don't have much chance to take it easy –</u> *Q16* <u>when someone tells you to do something you need to do it straightaway</u> – but at least we do have a very efficient air conditioning system compared with some kitchens.

Now let me tell you about some of the people you need to know. So as I said, <u>I'm Joy Parkins</u> *Q17*
<u>and I decide who does what during the day and how long they work for.</u> I'll be trying to get
you to work with as many different people in the kitchen as possible, so that you learn while
you're on the job. <u>One person whose name you must remember is David Field. If you injure</u> *Q18*
<u>yourself at all, even if it's really minor, you must report to him and he'll make sure the incident</u>
<u>is recorded and you get the appropriate treatment.</u> He's trained to give basic treatment to
staff himself, or he'll send you off somewhere else if necessary. <u>Then there's Dexter Wills –</u> *Q19*
<u>he's the person you need to see if you smash a plate or something like that.</u> Don't just leave
it and hope no one will notice – it's really important to get things noted and replaced or there
could be problems later. <u>And finally, there's Mike Smith. He's the member of staff who takes</u> *Q20*
<u>care of all the stores of perishables, so if you notice we're getting low in flour or sugar or</u>
<u>something, make sure you let him know so he can put in an order.</u>

OK, now the next thing …

SECTION 3

TRUDIE: OK, Stewart. We need to start planning our paper on public libraries. Have you
            thought of an angle yet?

STEWART: Well, there's so much we could look into. How libraries have changed over the
            centuries, for instance, or how different countries organise them. What do *you*
            think, Trudie?

TRUDIE: <u>Maybe we should concentrate on this country, and try and relate the changes in</u> *Q21*
            <u>libraries to external developments, like the fact that far more people can read than</u>
            <u>a century ago, and that the local population may speak lots of different languages.</u>

STEWART: We could include something about changes in the source of funding, too.

TRUDIE: Yes, but remember we're only supposed to write a short paper, so it's probably
            best if we don't go into funding in any detail.

STEWART: Right. Well, shall we just brainstorm a few ideas, to get started?

TRUDIE: OK. We obviously need to look at the impact of new technology, particularly the
            internet. Now that lots of books have been digitalised, people can access them
            from their own computers at home.

STEWART: And if everyone did that, libraries would be obsolete.

TRUDIE: Yes.

STEWART: <u>But the digitalised books that are available online for free are mostly out of</u> *Q22*
            <u>copyright, aren't they? And copyright in this country lasts for 70 years after the</u>
            <u>author dies. So you won't find the latest best-seller or up-to-date information.</u>

TRUDIE: <u>That's an important point.</u> Anyway, I find it hard to concentrate when I'm reading a
            long text on a screen. I'd much rather read a physical book. And it takes longer to
            read on a screen.

STEWART: Oh, I prefer it. I suppose it's just a personal preference.

TRUDIE: Mm. I expect that libraries will go on evolving in the next few years. Some have
            already become centres where community activities take place, like local clubs
            meeting there. I think that'll become even more common.

STEWART: I'd like to think so, and that they'll still be serving their traditional function, but I'm
            not so sure. There are financial implications, after all. <u>What I'm afraid will happen is</u> *Q23*
            <u>that books and magazines will all disappear, and there'll just be rows and rows of</u>
            <u>computers.</u> They won't look anything like the libraries we're used to.

TRUDIE: Well, we'll see.

TRUDIE:	I've just had an idea. Why don't we make an in-depth study of our local public library as background to our paper?
STEWART:	Yes, that'd be interesting, and raise all sorts of issues. Let's make a list of possible things we could ask about, then work out some sort of structure. <u>For instance, um, we could interview some of the staff, and find out whether the library has its own budget, or if that's controlled by the local council.</u>

Q24

TRUDIE:	And what their policies are. I know they don't allow food, but I'd love to find out what types of noise they ban – there always seems to be a lot of talking, but never music. I don't know if that's a policy or it just happens.
STEWART:	Ah, I've often wondered. <u>Then there are things like how the library is affected by employment laws. I suppose there are rules about working hours, facilities for staff, and so on.</u>

Q25

TRUDIE:	Right. <u>Then there are other issues relating to the design of the building and how customers use it. Like what measures does the library take to ensure their safety?</u> They'd need floor coverings that aren't slippery, and emergency exits, for instance. Oh, and another thing – <u>there's the question of the kind of insurance the library needs to have, in case anyone gets injured</u>.

Q26

Q27

STEWART:	Yes, that's something else to find out. You know something I've often wondered?
TRUDIE:	What's that?
STEWART:	Well, you know they've got an archive of local newspapers going back years? Well, <u>next to it they've got the diary of a well-known politician from the late 19th century</u>. I wonder why it's there. Do you know what his connection was with this area?

Q28

TRUDIE:	No idea. Let's add it to our list of things to find out. Oh, I've just thought – <u>you know people might ask in the library about local organisations, like sports clubs? Well, I wonder if they keep a database, or whether they just look online.</u>

Q29

STEWART:	Right. <u>I quite fancy finding out what the differences are between a library that's open to the public and one that's part of a museum, for example</u> – they must be very different.
TRUDIE:	Mmm. Then something else I'd like to know is …

Q30

SECTION 4

In public discussion of business, we take certain values for granted. Today I'm going to talk about four of them: collaboration, hard work, creativity and excellence. Most people would say they're all 'good things'. I'm going to suggest that's an over-simple view.

The trouble with these values is that they're theoretical concepts, removed from the reality of day-to-day business. <u>Pursue values by all means, but be prepared for what may happen as a result. They can actually cause damage, which is not at all the intention.</u> *Q31*

Business leaders generally try to do the right thing. But <u>all too often the right thing backfires, if those leaders adopt values without understanding and managing the side effects that arise</u>. The values can easily get in the way of what's actually intended. *Q32*

OK. So the first value I'm going to discuss is collaboration. Er, let me give you an example. <u>On a management training course I once attended, we were put into groups and had to construct a bridge across a stream</u>, using building blocks that we were given. The rule was that everyone in the team had to move at least one building block during the construction. This was intended to encourage teamwork. *Q33*

But it was really a job best done by one person. <u>The other teams tried to collaborate on</u>   *Q34*
<u>building the structure, and descended into confusion</u>, with everyone getting in each other's
way. Our team leader solved the challenge brilliantly. She simply asked everyone in the team
to move a piece a few centimetres, to comply with the rule, and then let the person in the
team with an aptitude for puzzles like this build it alone. We finished before any other team.
My point is that the task wasn't really suited to teamworking, so why make it one?

Teamwork can also lead to inconsistency – a common cause of poor sales. <u>In the case of</u>   *Q35*
<u>a smartphone that a certain company launched, one director wanted to target the business</u>
<u>market, and another demanded it was aimed at consumers. The company wanted both</u>
<u>directors to be involved, so gave the product a consumer-friendly name, but marketed it to</u>
<u>companies. The result was that it met the needs of neither group. It would have been better</u>
<u>to let one director or the other have his way, not both.</u>

Now industriousness, or hard work. It's easy to mock people who say they work hard: after
all, a hamster running around in a wheel is working hard – and getting nowhere. Of course
<u>hard work is valuable, but only when properly targeted. Otherwise it wastes the resources</u>   *Q36*
<u>that companies value most – time and energy. And that's bad for the organisation.</u>

There's a management model that groups people according to four criteria: clever, hard-
working, stupid and lazy. <u>Here 'lazy' means having a rational determination not to carry out</u>   *Q37*
<u>unnecessary tasks.</u> It doesn't mean trying to avoid work altogether. Most people display two
of these characteristics, and the most valuable people are those who are both clever and
lazy: they possess intellectual clarity, and they don't rush into making decisions. They come
up with solutions to save the time and energy spent by the stupid and hard-working group.
Instead of throwing more man-hours at a problem, the clever and lazy group looks for a more
effective solution.

Next we come to creativity. This often works well – creating an attention-grabbing TV
commercial, for example, might lead to increased sales. But it isn't *always* a good thing.
Some advertising campaigns are remembered for their creativity, without having any effect
on sales. <u>This happened a few years ago with the launch of a chocolate bar: subsequent</u>   *Q38*
<u>research showed that plenty of consumers remembered the adverts, but had no idea what</u>
<u>was being advertised.</u> The trouble is that the creator derives pleasure from coming up with
the idea, and wrongly assumes the audience for the campaign will share that feeling.

A company that brings out thousands of new products may *seem* more creative than a
company that only has a few, but it may be *too* creative, and make smaller profits. <u>Creativity</u>   *Q39*
<u>needs to be targeted, to solve a problem that the company has identified.</u> Just coming up with
more and more novel products isn't necessarily a good thing.

And finally, excellence. We all know companies that claim they 'strive for excellence', but
it takes a long time to achieve excellence. In business, being *first* with a product is more
profitable than having the *best* product. A major study of company performance compared
pioneers – that is, companies bringing out the *first* version of a particular product – with
followers, the companies that copied and improved on that product. <u>The study found that the</u>   *Q40*
<u>pioneers commanded an average market share of 29 percent, while the followers achieved</u>
<u>less than half that, only 13 percent</u> – even though their product might have been better.

Insisting on excellence in everything we do is time-consuming, wastes energy and leads
to losing out on opportunities. Sometimes, second-rate work is more worthwhile than
excellence. 'Make sure it's excellent' *sounds* like a good approach to business, but the 'just-
get-started' approach is likely to be more successful.

TEST 6

SECTION 1

MAN:	Good morning, Kenton Festival box office. How can I help you?
WOMAN:	Oh, good morning. I'm coming to Kenton for a few days' holiday next month, and a friend told me there's a festival. She gave me this number to find out about it.
MAN:	That's right, <u>the festival begins on the 16th of May</u> and goes on till the 19th.

Example

WOMAN: Oh, that's great. I'll be there from the 15th till the 19th. So could you tell me the programme, please?

MAN: Well, on the first day, there's the opening ceremony, in the town centre. People start gathering around 2 o'clock, to get a good place to see from, and <u>the events will start at 2.45</u>, and finish about 5.30.   **Q1**

WOMAN: OK, thanks. I'll make sure I get there early to get a good spot.

MAN: The festival will be officially opened by the mayor. He'll just speak for a few minutes, welcoming everyone to the festival. All the town councillors will be there, and of course lots of other people.

WOMAN: Right.

MAN: <u>Then there'll be a performance by a band.</u> Most years we have a children's choir, but this year the local army cadets offered to perform, and they're very good.   **Q2**

WOMAN: Uhuh.

MAN: <u>After that, a community group from the town will perform a play they've written themselves, just a short one. It's about Helen Tungate.</u> I don't know if you've heard of her?   **Q3**

WOMAN: I certainly have. <u>She was a scientist years ago.</u>   **Q4**

MAN: That's right. She was born in Kenton exactly 100 years ago, so we're celebrating her centenary.

WOMAN: I'm a biologist, so I've always been interested in her. I didn't realise she came from Kenton.

MAN: Yes. Well, all that will take place in the afternoon, and <u>later, as the sun sets, there'll be a firework display. You should go to the park to watch, as you'll get the best view from there, and the display takes place on the opposite side of the river.</u> It's always one of the most popular events in the festival.   **Q5**

WOMAN: Sounds great.

WOMAN: And what's happening on the other days?

MAN: There are several events that go on the whole time. For example, <u>the students of the art college have produced a number of videos, all connected with relationships between children and their grandparents</u>.   **Q6**

WOMAN: That sounds interesting. It makes a change from children and parents, doesn't it!

MAN: Exactly. Because the art college is in use for classes, throughout the festival, <u>the videos are being shown in Handsworth House.</u>   **Q7**

WOMAN: How do you spell the name?

MAN: H-A-N-D-S-W-O-R-T-H. Handsworth House. It's close to the Town Hall.

WOMAN: Right.

MAN: Now let me see, what else can I tell you about?

WOMAN: Are there any displays of ballet dancing? I'm particularly interested in that as I do it as a hobby.

MAN: There isn't any ballet, I'm afraid, but <u>there'll be a demonstration of traditional dances from all round the country</u>.   **Q8**

WOMAN:	Oh, that'd be nice. Where's that being held?
MAN:	It's in the market in the town centre – the outdoor one, not the covered market. And **Q9** it's on at 2 and 5 every afternoon of the festival, apart from the first day.
WOMAN:	Lovely. I'm interested in all kinds of dancing, so I'm sure I'll enjoy that!
MAN:	Mmm. I'm sure you will.
WOMAN:	And I'd really like to go to some concerts, if there are any.
MAN:	Yes, there are several. Three performed by professionals, and one by local children.
WOMAN:	And where is it being held?
MAN:	It's in the library, which is in Park Street. On the 18th, at 6.30 in the evening.
WOMAN:	I presume I'll need tickets for that.
MAN:	Yes, you can book online, or you can buy them when you arrive in Kenton, either at **Q10** the festival box office, or from any shops displaying our logo in the windows.
WOMAN:	Well, I think that'll keep me busy for the whole of my stay in Kenton. Thank you so much for all your help.
MAN:	You're welcome. I hope you enjoy your stay.
WOMAN:	Thank you. Goodbye.

SECTION 2

Right. I've now almost succeeded in finalising plans for our tour, so I'll bring you up to date with what I know.

As you know, we're flying first to Munich, on Monday the 4th.

The flight is at 11.30, so it's too early to have lunch at the airport. I suggest we meet there for **Q11** coffee at 10, which should give us plenty of time for breakfast before we leave home.

When we arrive in Munich, we'll be met at the airport by Claus Bauer. Claus works for a tour **Q12** operator, and he'll look after us for the time we'll be in Germany. He's already liaised with the managers of the theatres we're going to visit, and he's also arranged for an officer of the National Theatre in Munich to show us round the theatre one afternoon during our stay.

Now last time we discussed this trip, I didn't have the precise cost for hotel rooms, but now I have. The normal rate at the hotel where we're staying is 150 euros a night for a double **Q13** room. I'd hoped to get that down to 120 euros, but in fact I've been able to negotiate a rate of 110. That'll be reflected in the final payment which you'll need to make by the end of this week.

On Tuesday, the day after our arrival, I *had* hoped we could sit in on a rehearsal at one of the theatres, but unfortunately that's proved very difficult to arrange, so instead we'll have a coach trip to one of the amazing castles in the mountains south of Munich.

On Tuesday evening, we'll all have dinner together in a restaurant near our hotel. From talking to you all about your preferences, it was clear that a typical local restaurant would be too meat-oriented for some of you. Some of you suggested an Italian restaurant, but I must **Q14** confess that I decided to book a Lebanese one, as we have plenty of opportunities to go to an Italian restaurant at home.

On Wednesday afternoon, the director of the play we're going to see that evening will talk to **Q15** us at the theatre. She'll describe the whole process of producing a play, including how she chose the actors, and, as the play we're going to see is a modern one, how she worked with the playwright.

Right. Now I'd just like to make a few points about the plays we're going to see, partly because it might influence your choice of clothes to take with you!

The play we're seeing on Wednesday evening is a modern one, and we're going to the premiere, so it'll be quite a dressy occasion, though of course you don't *have* to dress formally. I gather it's rather a multimedia production, with amazing lighting effects and a soundtrack of electronic music, though unfortunately the playwright is ill and is unlikely to be able to attend.   *Q16*

On Thursday we're seeing a play that was first performed last year, when it was commissioned to mark a hundred years since the birth in the town of a well-known scientist. We're going to see a revival of that production, which aroused a lot of interest.   *Q17*

Friday's play will really make you think hard about what clothes to pack, as it'll be in the garden of a palace. It's a beautiful setting, but I'd better warn you, there won't be much protection from the wind.   *Q18*

On Saturday, we're going by coach to a theatre in another town, not far from Munich. This will be the opening of a drama festival, and the mayor and all the other dignitaries of the town will be attending. After the performance, the mayor is hosting a reception for all the audience, and there'll be a band playing traditional music of the region.   *Q19*

And after having a day off on Sunday, our final play is on Monday, and it's in the stunning setting of the old Town Hall, which dates back to the 14th century. The performance marks the fifty years that the lead actor has been on stage, and the play is the one where he made his first professional appearance, all those years ago.   *Q20*

And the day after that, we'll be flying back home. Now have you got any questions before I …

SECTION 3

BETH: Oh good morning. You must be James. I'm Beth Cartwright – please call me Beth.
JAMES: Thank you.
BETH: Now as this is your first tutorial since you started on the Scandinavian Studies course, I'd like to find out something about you. Why did you decide to take this course?
JAMES: Well, my mother is Danish, and although we always lived in England, she used to talk about her home a lot, and that made me want to visit Denmark. We hardly ever did, though – my mother usually went on her own. But whenever her relations or friends were in England they always came to see us.   *Q21*
BETH: I see. So I assume you already speak Danish, one of the languages you'll be studying.
JAMES: I can get by when I talk to people, though I'm not terribly accurate.
BETH: Now you probably know that you'll spend the third year of the course abroad. Have you had any thoughts about that?
JAMES: I'm really looking forward to it. And although Denmark seems the obvious place to go, because of my family connections, I'd love to spend the time in Iceland.
BETH: Oh, I'm sure it can be arranged. Do you have any plans for when you graduate? A lot of students go on to take a master's degree.
JAMES: I think the four years of the undergraduate course will be enough for me. I'm interested in journalism, and I quite like the idea of moving to Scandinavia and writing for magazines. I'd find that more creative than translating, which I suppose most graduates do.   *Q22*

BETH:	OK. Now how are you finding the courses you're taking this term, James?	
JAMES:	Well, I'm really enjoying the one on Swedish cinema.	
BETH:	<u>That'll continue next term, but the one on Scandinavian literature that's running at the moment will be replaced by more specialised courses.</u> Oh, and by the way, if you're interested in watching Danish television programmes – there's going to be a course on that the term after next.	Q23
JAMES:	That sounds good.	
BETH:	Have you started thinking about the literature paper that you have to write in the next few weeks?	
JAMES:	Yes, my first choice would be to do something on the Icelandic sagas.	
BETH:	Hmm. The trouble with that is that a lot of people choose that topic, and it can be difficult to get hold of the books you'll need. Why not leave that for another time?	
JAMES:	Right.	
BETH:	<u>You might find modern novels or 19th century playwrights interesting.</u>	
JAMES:	<u>I've read or seen several plays in translation, so that would be a good idea.</u>	Q24
BETH:	Fine. I'll put you down for that topic.	
JAMES:	Right. So what would you advise me to aim at in the paper?	
BETH:	First I suggest you avoid taking one writer and going into a great deal of detail. That approach certainly has its place, but <u>I think you first need to get an understanding of the literature in the context of the society in which it was produced – who it was written for, how it was published, and so on.</u> I also think that's more fruitful than placing it within the history of the genre.	Q25
JAMES:	OK, that sounds reasonable.	

JAMES:	Could I ask for some advice about writing the paper I'm working on about the Vikings? I have to do that this week, and I'm a bit stuck.	
BETH:	Of course. Have you decided yet what to write about?	
JAMES:	No, I haven't. There's so much that seems interesting – Viking settlement in other countries, trade, mythology…	
BETH:	Well, <u>what I suggest is that you read an assignment a student wrote last year</u>, which is kept in the library. It's short and well focused, and I'm sure you'll find it helpful. I'll give you the details in a moment. Textbooks usually cover so many topics, it can be very difficult to choose just one.	Q26
JAMES:	OK. I've got a DVD of the film about the Vikings that came out earlier this year. Should I watch that again?	
BETH:	If it's the one I am thinking of, hmm, I'd ignore it – it's more fantasy than reality. But <u>I've got a recording of a documentary that you should watch</u>. It makes some interesting and provocative points, which I think will help you to focus your topic.	Q27
JAMES:	Right.	
JAMES:	<u>So then should I work out an outline?</u>	Q28
BETH:	<u>Yes. Just headings for different sections, at this stage.</u> And <u>then you should start looking for suitable articles and books to draw on, and take notes</u> which you organise according to those headings.	Q29
JAMES:	I see.	
BETH:	<u>Then put short phrases and sentences as bullet points under each heading.</u> Make sure that this skeleton makes sense and flows properly, before writing up the paper in full.	Q30
JAMES:	OK. Thanks, that's very helpful.	

SECTION 4

Over the years, attitudes towards workers have changed considerably. After all, there was a time when workers had no rights at all, and laboured in appalling conditions. Conditions have improved a lot, but conflict in the workplace is still common. And human resources managers nowadays need to be able to deal with it when necessary.

What is conflict in the workplace? Definitions vary, but I'm taking it to refer to a whole range of behaviours that the victim finds unacceptable, from minor, harmless arguments to – at the opposite extreme – physical violence. Much of this is covered by the term bullying, by which I mean one or more people behaving abusively or aggressively against another who is in a weaker position. Although all behaviour like this is a form of conflict, not all conflict can be described in these terms. *Q31*

As with all human behaviour, there are numerous reasons for it. But often it's caused by someone who feels the need to show their superiority over someone else, in order to feel that they aren't at the lowest level in a hierarchy or a group of people. *Q32*

In some cases one person simply dislikes the other, on the basis that the personality of one is in some way incompatible with that of the other person. A general habit of optimism in one person could make them intolerant of a colleague who's constantly pessimistic – not that that justifies treating them badly, of course. *Q33*

Some conflicts arise when people are more interested in promoting themselves and their team than in the company as a whole. These conflicts are called 'structural', and could come about, for example, when a sales team believe they are the only people in the business who do any useful work, and look down on behind-the-scenes administrators. *Q34*

Conflict obviously affects the individuals concerned – the situation is likely to be very stressful for victims, resulting in their absence from work, possibly for months. For the company, if no effort is made to deal with conflict, it can spiral out of control, and even lead to the breakdown of the business. *Q35*

Some interesting work with chief executives – CEOs – has uncovered some of the reasons why they may treat colleagues badly. Many CEOs combine two opposing characteristics: confidence – that is, the belief that they're capable of great achievements – with a high level of anxiety, a fear of missing targets, whether set by themselves or by the directors of the company. This combination can make them respond badly to anyone who questions their decisions. *Q36*

In a high pressure work environment, such characteristics become problematic. And it's particularly difficult to tackle the situation where colleagues, managers and board members are all trying to achieve their own visions. When they can't agree on strategic issues and on where they see the business going, there are real problems. *Q37*

For managers at lower levels within the organisation, it might seem that an autocratic form of management – where the chief executive gives orders and everyone else has to obey – would see more conflict than others. Interestingly, though, a company with a more democratic business model, can suffer *more*, when uncertainty about who to report to leads to conflicting demands. *Q38*

Now I'll say a little about dealing with the type of conflict that has harmful effects. Of course the ideal is to prevent it arising in the first place. A good manager, at any level, will make efforts to earn the respect of the people they work with, particularly those who report to them. That will involve politeness in all communications, and treating them as equals who happen to have a different role within the organisation. *Q39*

Sometimes, of course, conflict does occur, and can get out of hand. In such cases the human resources department often gets involved. However, <u>if one of the parties in a conflict sees human resources as simply a mouthpiece for the chief executive, then an external mediator might be able to help</u>. By talking to both sides, and trying to find the truth of what's been happening, they can build a clear picture of the situation, and give feedback that both sides will accept, precisely *because* they're independent.

Q40

SECTION 1

SUSIE:	Hello?
PAUL:	Hi, Susie, it's Paul here. How are you? Enjoying your new job? You're working at the library, aren't you?
SUSIE:	Yes. I started when <u>the library re-opened a month ago</u>. It's great.
PAUL:	Actually Carol and I have been meaning to join for a while.
SUSIE:	Oh, you should. It doesn't cost anything, and the new library has all sorts of facilities. It's not just a place where you borrow books. For instance, there's an area with comfortable seats where you can sit and read the magazines they have there. Some people spend the whole morning there.
PAUL:	Mmm. Wish I had that amount of time to spend!
SUSIE:	Yes, you must be pretty busy at present, with the children and everything?
PAUL:	We are, yes. But we're hoping to get away this summer. We're thinking of going to Greece.
SUSIE:	Well, <u>we've got a much larger section of the library devoted to travel books now</u>, so you should come and have a look. I can't remember if there's anything specifically on Greece, but I should think so.
PAUL:	OK. Now Carol's organising a project for the history class she teaches at school – it's about life in the town a hundred years ago. Do you have anything that might be useful?
SUSIE:	Yes, actually <u>we've now got a new section with materials on the history of the town and surrounding region</u>.
PAUL:	Right. I'll tell her. You can't always find that sort of thing on the internet. Now in the old library there used to be a separate room with reference books. It was a really nice quiet room.
SUSIE:	Yes. We've put those books in the main part of the library now, but <u>we do have a room called the community room. It can be hired out for meetings, but at other times people can use it to study</u>.
PAUL:	I might use that. It's hard to find anywhere quiet at home sometimes.
SUSIE:	I can't remember how old your son and daughter are … <u>we've introduced a special section of fiction written specially for teenagers</u>, but they might be a bit young for that?
PAUL:	Yes, they would be.

Example

Q1

Q2

Q3

Q4

SUSIE:	Well, we do have lots of activities for younger children.
PAUL:	Yes?
SUSIE:	For example <u>we have a Science Club. At the next meeting, they're going to be doing experiments with stuff that everyone has in the kitchen</u> – sugar and flour and so on.

Q5

PAUL:	They might be interested, yes.	
SUSIE:	And we have a competition for children called Reading Challenge. That doesn't begin until after the end of term. They have to read six books, and they get a certificate if they manage it.	
PAUL:	So that gives them something to do while they're on holiday, instead of getting bored.	
SUSIE:	That's the idea. And there's special activities for adults too. <u>On Friday we have a local author called Tanya Streep who's going to be talking about her new novel. It's called 'Catch the Mouse' and she based the story on a crime that actually took place here years ago.</u>	Q6
PAUL:	Right. We're not free on Friday, but I'll look out for the book.	
SUSIE:	Now this probably isn't for you, but <u>we do have IT support available for members. We get quite a few older people coming along who are wanting to get up to speed with computer technology. It's on Tuesday mornings – they don't need to make an appointment or anything, they just turn up.</u>	Q7
PAUL:	Well, my mother might be interested, I'll let her know.	
SUSIE:	OK. <u>And there's another service which you wouldn't expect from a library, which is a free medical check-up. The hospital arranges for someone to come along and measure the level of sugar in your blood, and they check cholesterol levels at the same time.</u>	Q8
PAUL:	<u>Really</u>?	
SUSIE:	<u>Yes, but that's only for the over-60s</u>, so you wouldn't qualify.	
PAUL:	OK. Well, I'll tell my mother, she might be interested.	
SUSIE:	What other information … well, <u>we do have a little shop with things like wallcharts and greetings cards, and also stamps</u> so you can post the cards straightaway, which is really useful.	Q9
PAUL:	Yeah. Well, I'll bring the children round at the weekend and we'll join. Oh, one more thing – I'll be bringing the car, <u>is there parking available?</u>	Q10
SUSIE:	<u>Yes, and it's free in the evening and at weekends.</u>	
PAUL:	Perfect. Well, thanks, Susie see you …	

SECTION 2

In this session in your training day we're going to look at some of the more specialised holidays we offer at BC Travel. Now, the travel business is very competitive and it's important to be aware of how the market's changing and developing. In terms of age groups, <u>the over-65s are</u>   Q11 & <u>an important market, and one that's increasing steadily year on year</u>. The fewest holidays are   Q12 taken by the 31 to 42-year-olds, and that figure shows no sign of rising. The biggest market at present is still the youngest group, the 16 to 30s, but this group's also seen the biggest drop over the last few years, <u>whereas there's a noticeable growth in the number of holidays taken</u>   Q11 & <u>by the 55 to 64-year-olds</u>. As far as the 43 to 54-year-olds are concerned, bookings there are   Q12 steady, but I have to say we haven't seen the increase we expected.

One trend we're noticing with nearly all age groups is the growing popularity of holidays in which clients do some kind of specialised activity. I'm not talking here about adventure holidays, where clients take part in high-risk activities like white water rafting just for the thrill of it. Activity holidays usually involve rather less high-risk sports, or things like art and music. They're not necessarily cheaper than ordinary holidays, often the opposite, in fact. But <u>they</u>   Q13 & <u>do often take place outside the main tourist centres, which gives an opportunity for clients</u>   Q14 <u>to find out more about the local people and customs</u>, and many say this is one of the most positive features of these holidays. Of course, they offer the chance to develop a new skill or

talent, <u>but clients often say that more than this, it's the chance to create lasting relationships</u>   *Q13 &*
<u>with other like-minded people that's the main draw.</u>   *Q14*

Let me give you some examples of BC Travel activity holidays. Our painting holidays take place in four different centres in France and Italy and they're very popular with clients of all abilities from beginners onwards. <u>We've got an excellent team of artists to lead the classes –</u>   *Q15*
<u>some of them have been with us from the start, and five additional ones will be joining us this</u>
<u>year</u> so that we can offer a greater number of classes in each centre.

As far as cooking holidays are concerned, I know <u>a lot of agents offer holidays where clients</u>   *Q16*
<u>cook recipes related to one particular country, usually the one they're staying in, but we focus</u>
<u>on dishes from a great many different ones.</u> Apart from that you'll find the usual emphasis on good quality, organic ingredients – that's more or less a given nowadays – and there are generally some meat-free recipes included.

Our photography holidays take place in a wide range of countries from Iceland to Vietnam, and clients have the opportunity to see some stunning scenery. Groups are small, no more than eight, so <u>clients can have one-on-one tuition during the holiday,</u> and excursions are   *Q17*
arranged with fully-trained guides. At the end of each holiday an exhibition is held of the photographs taken so that clients can see one another's work and receive valuable feedback from the tutor.

Finally, let me tell you about our fitness holidays. In Ireland and Italy we run one-week general fitness classes for all ages and levels of fitness. Clients start the course with a consultation with a trainer, and together they draw up an individual programme. As well as improving general fitness, <u>clients find that they end up losing much of the stress they've built</u>   *Q18*
<u>up in their daily lives.</u>

<u>In Greece, we have a two-week holiday for clients who want to do something about their</u>   *Q19*
<u>weight.</u> This has all the features you'd expect, like a personalised diet programme, but one of its most popular features is that the exercise classes are all held on the beach. People say it's far preferable to being in a gym.

Finally, we offer several holidays in Morocco. One very popular one is the mountain biking holiday. Bikes are provided and there are different routes according to people's ability. <u>We</u>   *Q20*
<u>offer one which is tailored to the needs of families</u>, which is particularly popular.

OK, so that's about all the time I have today, so thank you very much ...

SECTION 3

NATALIE: Dave, I'm worried about our case study. I've done a bit of reading, but I'm not sure what's involved in actually writing a case study – I missed the lecture where Dr Baker talked us through it.

DAVE: OK, well it's quite straightforward. We've got our focus – that's tourism at the Horton Castle site. And you said you'd done some reading about it.

NATALIE: Yes, I found some articles and made notes of the main points.

DAVE: <u>Did you remember to keep a record of where you got the information from?</u>   *Q21*

NATALIE: Sure. I know what a pain it is when you forget that.

DAVE: OK, so we can compare what we've read. Then we have to decide on a particular problem or need at our site. And then think about who we're going to interview to get more information.

NATALIE: OK. So who'd that be? <u>The people who work there?</u> And presumably some of the tourists too?　　　　　　　　　　　　　　　　　　　　　　　　　　　　　　Q22

DAVE: Yes, both those groups. So we'll have to go to the site to do that, I suppose. But we might also do some of our interviewing away from the site – <u>we could even contact</u>　　Q23 <u>some people here in the city, like administrators involved in overseeing tourism.</u>

NATALIE: OK. So we'll need to think about our interview questions and fix times and places for the meetings. It's all going to take a lot of time.

DAVE: Mmm. And if we can, we should ask our interviewees if they can bring along some numerical data that we can add to support our findings.

NATALIE: And photographs?

DAVE: I think we have plenty of those already. <u>But Dr Baker also said we have to establish</u>　　Q24 <u>with our interviewees whether we can identify them in our case study, or whether</u> <u>they want to be anonymous.</u>

NATALIE: Oh, I wouldn't have thought of that. OK, once we've got all this information, I suppose we have to analyse it.

DAVE: Yes, put it all together and choose what's relevant to the problem we're focusing on, and <u>analyse that carefully to find out if we can identify any trends or regularities</u>　　Q25 there. That's the main thing at this stage, rather than concentrating on details or lots of facts.

NATALIE: OK. And then once we've analysed that, what next?

DAVE: Well, then we need to think about what we do with the data we've selected to make it as clear as possible to our readers. Things like graphs, or tables, or charts…

NATALIE: Right.

DAVE: Then the case study itself is mostly quite standard; we begin by presenting the problem, and giving some background, then go through the main sections, but the thing that surprised me is that <u>in a normal report we'd end with some suggestions</u>　　Q26 <u>to deal with the problem or need we identified, but in a case study we end up with a</u> <u>question or a series of questions to our readers, and they decide what ought to be</u> <u>done.</u>

NATALIE: Oh, I hadn't realised that.

NATALIE: So basically, the problem we're addressing in our case study of the Horton Castle site is why so few tourists are visiting it. And we'll find out more from our interviews, but I did find one report on the internet that suggested that one reason might be because as far as transport goes, access is difficult.

DAVE: I read that too, but that report was actually written ten years ago, when the road there was really bad, but that's been improved now. And <u>I think there's plenty of</u>　　Q27 <u>fascinating stuff there for a really good day out, but you'd never realise it from the</u> <u>castle website – maybe that's the problem.</u>

NATALIE: <u>Yes, it's really dry and boring.</u>

DAVE: I read somewhere a suggestion that what the castle needs is a visitor centre. So we could have a look for some information about that on the internet. What would we need to know?

NATALIE: Well, who'd use it for a start. It'd be good to know what categories the visitors fell into too, like school parties or retired people, but I think we'd have to talk to staff to get that information.

DAVE: OK. And as we're thinking of suggesting a visitor centre we'd also have to look at potential problems. I mean, obviously it wouldn't be cheap to set up.

NATALIE: No, but it could be a really good investment. <u>And as it's on a historical site it'd need</u>　　Q28 <u>to get special planning permission, I expect. That might be hard.</u>

DAVE: Right, especially as the only possible place for it would be at the entrance, and that's right in front of the castle.

NATALIE: Mmm.

DAVE: But it could be a good thing for the town of Horton. At present it's a bit of a ghost town. <u>Once they've left school and got any skills or qualifications, the young people all get out as fast as they can to get jobs in the city, and the only people left are children and those who've retired.</u> *Q29*

NATALIE: Right. Something else we could investigate would be the potential damage that tourists might cause to the castle site, I mean their environmental impact. At present the tourists can just wander round wherever they want, but <u>if numbers increase, there might have to be some restrictions, like sticking to marked ways. And there'd need to be guides and wardens around to make sure these were enforced.</u> *Q30*

DAVE: Yes, we could look at that too. OK, well …

SECTION 4

OK, so we've been looking at how man-made changes in our environment can affect wildlife. Now I'll discuss a particular example. Let's take a look at mercury. Mercury's one of the 120 or so elements that make up all matter, and it has the symbol Hg. It's a shiny, silvery substance. You may have seen it in old-fashioned thermometers, but it's not used much for domestic purposes now because it's highly toxic.

But the problem is that the amount of mercury in the environment's increasing. The main reason for this is the power plants used to produce electricity. The main source of energy that most of them use is still coal, and when it's burned it releases mercury into the atmosphere. Some of this gets deposited into lakes and rivers, and if it's ingested by a fish it's not excreted, it stays in the fish's body and it enters the food chain. So it's been known for some time that birds which eat fish may be affected, but <u>what wasn't known until quite recently is that those that eat insects can also be affected</u>. *Q31*

So a woman called Claire Varian-Ramos is doing some research on how this is affecting birds.

And rather than looking at how many birds are actually killed by mercury poisoning, she's looking for more subtle sub-effects. And <u>these may be to do with the behaviour of the birds, or with the effect of mercury on the way their brain works, so whether it leads to problems with memory, for example</u>. And she's particularly focusing on the effects of mercury on bird song. <u>Now, the process of song learning happens at a particular stage in the birds' development, and what you may not know is that a young bird seems to acquire this skill by listening to the songs produced by its father</u>, rather than by any other bird. *Q32* *Q33*

And Varian-Ramos has already found in her research that <u>if young male birds are exposed to mercury, if they eat food contaminated with mercury, then the songs they produce aren't as complex as those produced by other birds</u>. So quite low-level exposure to mercury is likely to have an impact on male birds in a natural situation, because it can mean that they're less attractive to female birds, and so <u>it can affect their chances of reproduction</u>. *Q34* *Q35*

Now the way she's carrying out this research is worth thinking about. She's using a mixture of studies using birds kept in laboratories, and studies carried out outdoors in the wild. <u>The lab-based studies have the advantage that you don't get all the variables you would in a natural setting, so the experimenter has a much higher level of control</u>, and that means they can be more confident about their results in some ways. And of course they don't have to worry about going out and finding the birds in order to observe them. *Q36*

So what are the implications here for humans? Well, because many birds are migratory, they may be transporting mercury far from contaminated sites. For example, it's been found that ducks who'd been feeding at a contaminated site were later shot by hunters over a thousand kilometres away, and presumably eaten. But these birds likely had mercury levels high enough to warrant concern for human consumption. *Q37*

In addition, going back to song learning by birds, we saw that this may be affected by mercury contamination. Well, we also know that in humans, mercury causes developmental delays in the acquisition of language, and in fact this process is very similar in the brain regions it involves and even the genes that are involved. But mercury contamination has other important implications for humans as well. It's now known that an unborn child can be affected if the food eaten by its mother contains high levels of mercury, and these effects can be quite substantial. *Q38* *Q39*

In the end, it comes down to whether more value is placed on human economic wellbeing or environmental wellbeing. It's true there are new regulations for mercury emissions from power plants, but these will need billions of dollars to implement, and increase costs for everyone. Some argue that's too much to pay to protect wildlife. But as we've seen, the issues go beyond that, and I think it's an issue we need to consider very carefully. *Q40*

TEST 8

SECTION 1

BOB: Hello, Pembroke Cycling Holidays, Bob speaking.

MARGARET: Oh hello. I've seen your advert for people to lead cycle trips. Are you the right person to speak to?

BOB: Yes, I am. Could I have your name, please?

MARGARET: It's Margaret Smith. *Example*

BOB: Are you looking for a permanent job, Margaret? *Q1*

MARGARET: No, temporary. I've got a permanent job starting in a few months' time, and I want to do something else until then.

BOB: What work do you do?

MARGARET: This will probably sound crazy – I used to be a lawyer, and then I made a complete career change and I'm going to be a doctor. I've just finished my training. *Q2*

BOB: Right. And have you had any experience of leading cycle trips?

MARGARET: Yes, I've led several bike tours in Africa. The trip to India that I had arranged to lead next month has now been cancelled, so when I saw you were advertising for tour leaders, I decided to apply. *Q3*

BOB: OK. Now we normally have two or three leaders on a trip, depending on the size of the group. Some tours are for very experienced cyclists, but we've got a tour coming up soon in Spain, which is proving so popular we need an additional leader. It's a cycling holiday for families. Would that suit you?

MARGARET: It certainly would. I enjoy working with children, and I probably need some more experience before I go on a really challenging trip.

BOB: That tour includes several teenagers: have you worked with that age group before?

MARGARET: Yes, I'm a volunteer worker in a youth club, where I help people to improve their cycling skills. Before that I helped out in a cycling club where I taught beginners. *Q4*

BOB:	Well that's great. Now the trip I mentioned is just for a fortnight, but there might be the possibility of leading other tours after that. Would that fit in with your plans?	
MARGARET:	That'd be fine. <u>I'll be free for five months. My job is due to start on October the 2nd, and I'm available from May the 1st until late September.</u>	Q5
BOB:	Good. Now is there anything I need to know about the food you eat? We usually have one or two people in the group who don't eat meat, or have some sort of food allergy, so we're always very careful about that.	
MARGARET:	Yes, <u>I'm allergic to cheese</u>. Would that be a problem?	Q6
BOB:	No, as long as we have enough notice, we can deal with that.	
MARGARET:	That's great.	

MARGARET:	It sounds really interesting – would you like me to fill in an application form?	
BOB:	Yes, please. Where should I post it to?	
MARGARET:	Could you send it to <u>27 Arbuthnot Place – A-R-B-U-T-H-N-O-T – Place, Dumfries.</u>	Q7
BOB:	<u>And what's the postcode, please</u>?	
MARGARET:	<u>DG7 4PH.</u>	Q8
BOB:	Was that P Papa or B Bravo?	
MARGARET:	P Papa.	
BOB:	Got that. If you could return the application form by Friday this week, <u>we can interview you on Tuesday next week</u>. Say half past two. Would that be possible for you?	Q9
MARGARET:	Yes, it's fine. You're quite a long way from where I live, so I'll drive over on Monday. Should I bring anything to the interview?	
BOB:	We'll have your application form, of course, but we'll need to see any certificates you've got that are relevant, in cycling, first aid, or whatever.	
MARGARET:	OK.	
BOB:	<u>And at the interview we'd like to find out about your experience of being a tour guide, so could you prepare a ten-minute talk about that, please?</u> You don't need slides or any complicated equipment – just some notes.	Q10
MARGARET:	Right. I'll start thinking about that straightaway!	
BOB:	Good. Well, we'll look forward to receiving your application form, and we'll contact you to confirm the interview.	
MARGARET:	Thanks very much.	
BOB:	Thank you, Margaret. Goodbye.	
MARGARET:	Bye.	

SECTION 2

Welcome to this podcast about the Sheepmarket, which is one of the oldest parts of the city. As its name suggests, there was originally a market here where farmers brought their sheep, but now it's been redeveloped into a buzzing, vibrant area of the city, which is also home to one of the city's fastest-growing communities. The nearby university has always meant the area's popular with students, who come in to enjoy the lively nightlife, but <u>now graduates embarking on careers in the worlds of fashion and design are buying up the new apartments recently built here to replace the small houses where the market workers used to live.</u>   Q11

<u>The narrow old side streets are great places for finding original pictures, jewellery and ceramics</u> which won't break the bank, as well as local produce like fruit and vegetables. There's also lots of pavement cafes where you can have a coffee and watch tourists from all   Q12

over the world go by. The oldest buildings in the area are on the main streets, including the city's first department store, built in the 1880s, which is still open today.

The Sheepmarket is a centre for fashion, and there's a policy of encouraging new young designers. The Young Fashion competition is open to local young people who are passionate about fashion. <u>This year they've been asked to design an outfit based on ideas from the music and technology that's part of their everyday life</u>, using both natural and man-made fibres. The garments will be judged by a panel of experts and fashion designers, and the winning entries will be modelled at a special gala evening.

Q13

Parking at the Sheepmarket is easy. There are plenty of pay and display car parking spaces on the roadsides which are fine if you just want to stay for an hour or two, but if you want to spend the day there it's better to park in one of the four underground car parks. It's not expensive and <u>if you can present a receipt from one of the local stores, you'll not be charged at all</u>. After six pm many of the car parks have a flat rate which varies but it is usually very reasonable.

Q14

The Sheepmarket is one of the main centres for art and history in the whole of the country. If you look at our map, you'll see some of the main attractions there. Most visitors start from Crawley Road, at the bottom of the map. <u>The Reynolds House is one of the oldest houses in the city, and is open to the public. It's on the north side of Crawley Road, next to the footpath that leads to the public gardens.</u>

Q15

The area's particularly interesting for its unusual sculptures. <u>'The Thumb' is just what its name suggests, but it's about 10 metres high. You'll see it on Hill Road, across the road from the Bank.</u>

Q16

<u>The Museum's got a particularly fine collection of New Zealand landscapes. It's on the east side of the Sheepmarket, on City Road. It's on the other side of the road from the public gardens, immediately facing the junction with Hill Road.</u>

Q17

<u>The Contemporary Art Gallery is on a little road that leads off Station Square, not far from the public gardens. The road ends at the gallery – it doesn't go anywhere else.</u> That's open every day except Mondays.

Q18

<u>The Warner Gallery specialises in 19th-century art. It's on City Road, near the junction with Crawley Road, on the same side of the road as the public gardens.</u> It's open on weekdays from 9 to 5, and entry is free.

Q19

<u>Finally, if you're interested in purchasing high quality artwork, the place to go is Nucleus. You need to go from Crawley Road up through Station Square and east along Hill Road until you get to a small winding road turning off. Go up there and it's on your right – if you get to City Road you've gone too far.</u>

Q20

SECTION 3

KATIE: Joe, you know I'm giving a presentation in our film studies class next week?

JOE: Yes.

KATIE: Well, could we discuss it? I could do with getting someone else's opinion.

JOE: Of course, Katie. What are you going to talk about?

KATIE: It's about film adaptations of Shakespeare's plays. I've got very interested in all the different approaches that film directors take.

JOE: Uhuh.

KATIE: So I thought I'd start with Giannetti, who's a professor of film and literature, and in one   Q21
of his books he came up with a straightforward classification of film adaptations based
on how faithful they are to the original plays and novels.

JOE: Right.

KATIE: I've already made some notes on that, so I just need to sort those out before the
presentation. I thought that next I'd ask the class to come up with the worst examples   Q22
of Shakespeare adaptations that they've seen, and to say why. That should be more
fun than having their favourite versions.

JOE: Yes, I can certainly think of a couple!

KATIE: Right. Next I want to talk about Rachel Malchow. I came across something on the
internet about her work on film adaptations, and I was thinking of showing some film
clips to illustrate her ideas.

JOE: Will you have enough time, though? Both to prepare and during the presentation?
After all, I doubt if you'll be able to find all the clips you want.

KATIE: Hmm. Perhaps you're right. OK, well, I'd better do some slides instead, saying how   Q23
various films relate to what she says. That should encourage discussion.

JOE: Mmm.

KATIE: Next I want to say something about how plays may be chosen for adaptation because   Q24
they're concerned with issues of the time when the film is made.

JOE: You mean things like patriotism, or the role of governments?

KATIE: Exactly. It's quite tricky, but I've got a few ideas I'd like to discuss.

KATIE: And finally I want to talk about a few adaptations that I think illustrate a range of
approaches, and make some comments on them. Do you know the Japanese film
Ran?

JOE: I haven't seen it. It was based on Shakespeare's *King Lear*, wasn't it?

KATIE: That's right. It was a very loose adaptation, using the same situation and story, but   Q25
moving it to 16th century Japan instead of 16th century Britain. So for example the
king's daughters become sons, because in Japanese culture at that time, women
couldn't succeed to the throne.

JOE: OK. I hope you're going to talk about the 1993 film of *Much Ado About Nothing*. I think
that's one of the best Shakespeare films. It really brings the play to life, doesn't it?

KATIE: Yes, I agree. And I think filming it in Italy, where the play is set, makes you see what   Q26
life was like at the time of the play.

JOE: Absolutely. Right, what's next?

KATIE: Er, next, I thought *Romeo & Juliet*, the 1996 film, which moves the action into the   Q27
present day.

JOE: Yes, it worked really well, I thought – changing the two feuding families in the original
to two competing business empires, even though they're speaking in the English of the
original play.

KATIE: You'd expect it would sound really bizarre, but I found I soon got used to it.

JOE: Me too.

KATIE: Then I thought I'd include a real Hollywood film, one that's intended to appeal to a
mass commercial audience.

JOE: There must be quite a number of those.

KATIE: Yes, but I've picked the 1996 film of *Hamlet*. It included every line of the text, but   Q28
it's more like a typical action hero movie – there are loads of special effects, but no
unifying interpretation of the play.

JOE: All show and no substance.

KATIE: Exactly. Then there's *Prospero's Books*, based on *The Tempest*. That was really   Q29
innovative, from a stylistic point of view.

JOE: Didn't it include dance and singing and animation, as well as live actors?
KATIE: Yes, it did. I also want to mention *Looking for Richard*. Did you ever see it?   *Q30*
JOE: No, but I've read about it. It was a blend of a documentary with a few scenes from *Richard III*, wasn't it?
KATIE: That's right. It's more a way of looking into how people nowadays connect with the playwright – the play is really just the starting point. And that'll be where I finish.
JOE: Well, it sounds as though it'll be very interesting.

SECTION 4

This lecture will be about the science of acoustics, the study of sound, in relation to urban environments such as cities. As an acoustic engineer myself, I think this is an area where we're likely to see great changes. In the past, researching urban soundscapes was simple. We measured levels of sound in decibels, so I used to take my sound meter and I measured the noise somewhere, and then I might ask a sample of people to say at what level the sound became annoying.

With data like this, acoustic engineers have been able to build up what we call noise maps, maps of the sound environment. But actually these aren't a lot of use. What they do show is that the highest noise levels are generally on roads – well, that's not really very surprising. But there's quite a lot going on that these maps don't show, because they can't capture the complex way that sound varies over time. So they ignore important issues such as the   *Q31* noise someone might hear from the open windows or gardens of their neighbours, and this sort of noise can be quite significant in summer. We don't have any databases on this sort of information. As well as that, these records of sound levels take no account of the fact that people vary in their perceptions of noise – so someone like me with years of working in acoustics might be very different from you in that regard.

But anyway, even though these noise maps are fairly crude, they've been useful in providing   *Q32* information and raising awareness that noise matters, we need to deal with it and so it's a political matter. And that's important – we need rules and regulations because noise can cause all sorts of problems.

Those of you who are city-dwellers know that things go on 24 hours a day, so city-dwellers often suffer from interrupted sleep. It's also known that noise can lead to a rise in levels of stress, due to physical changes in the body affecting the composition of the blood. And there are other problems as well, for instance if schoolchildren don't have a quiet place to study,   *Q33* their work will suffer.

Now, one problem with decibel measurement is that it doesn't differentiate between different types of noise. Some types of sounds that most people would probably think of as nice and   *Q34* relaxing might well score quite highly in decibel levels – think of the sound made by a fountain in a town square, for example. That's not necessarily something that we'd want to control or reduce. So maybe researchers should consider these sorts of sounds in urban design. This is going to be tricky because just measuring decibel levels isn't going to help us here. Instead,   *Q35* many researchers are using social science techniques, studying people's emotional response to sound by using questionnaires and so on.

So what exactly do people want to hear in an urban environment? Some recent interdisciplinary research has come out with results that at first sight seem contradictory – a   *Q36* city needs to have a sense of activity, so it needs to be lively, with sounds like the clack of high heels on a pavement or the hiss of a coffee machine, but these mustn't be too intrusive, because at the same time we need to be able to relax.

One of the major problems in achieving this will be getting architects and town planners to use the research. Apart from studying the basics of acoustics, these people receive very little training in this area. But in fact they should be regarding sound as an opportunity to add to the experience of urban living, whereas at present they tend to see it as something to be avoided or reduced as far as possible, or something that's just a job for engineers like the street drainage system.

Q37

What's needed is for noise in cities to be regarded as an aesthetic quality, as something that has the qualities of an art form. If we acknowledge this, then we urgently need to know what governs it and how designers can work with it. We need to develop a complex understanding of many factors. What is the relationship between sound and culture? What can we learn from disciplines such as psychology about the way that sound interacts with human development and social relationships, and the way that sound affects our thought and feelings? Can we learn anything from physics about the nature of sound itself?

Q38

Q39

Today's powerful technologies can also help us. To show us their ideas and help us to imagine the effect their buildings will have, architects and town planners already use virtual reality – but these programs are silent. In the future such programs could use realistic sounds, meaning that soundscapes could be explored before being built. So hopefully, using the best technology we can lay our hands on, the city of the future will be a pleasure to the ears as well as the eyes.

Q40

Listening and Reading Answer Keys

TEST 5

LISTENING

Section 1, Questions 1–10

1	mountains
2	horse
3	garden(s)
4	lunch
5	map
6	experience
7	Ratchesons
8	helmet
9	shops
10	267

Section 2, Questions 11–20

11	A
12	A
13	C
14	C

15&16 *IN EITHER ORDER*

	A
	E
17	F
18	C
19	D
20	B

Section 3, Questions 21–30

21	B
22	C
23	C
24	budget
25	employment
26	safety
27	insurance
28	diary
29	database
30	museum

Section 4, Questions 31–40

31	damage
32	side effects
33	bridge
34	confusion
35	smartphone
36	resources
37	unnecessary/not necessary
38	chocolate bar
39	problem
40	market share

If you score …

0–15	16–24	25–40
you are unlikely to get an acceptable score under examination conditions and we recommend that you spend a lot of time improving your English before you take IELTS.	you may get an acceptable score under examination conditions but we recommend that you think about having more practice or lessons before you take IELTS.	you are likely to get an acceptable score under examination conditions but remember that different institutions will find different scores acceptable.

READING

Reading Passage 1, Questions 1–14

1 G
2 D
3 B
4 A
5 F
6 D
7 E
8 C
9 FALSE
10 NOT GIVEN
11 TRUE
12 TRUE
13 FALSE
14 FALSE

Reading Passage 2, Questions 15–27

15 research
16 survey
17 mix
18 updates
19 information
20 reputation
21 self(-)employed
22 average
23 agreement
24 checks
25 train
26 freedom
27 congestion

Reading Passage 3, Questions 28–40

28 myths
29 levers
30 tools
31 F
32 E
33 B
34 D
35 A
36 palace
37 trades
38 water
39 techniques
40 children

If you score ...

0–19	20–31	32–40
you are unlikely to get an acceptable score under examination conditions and we recommend that you spend a lot of time improving your English before you take IELTS.	you may get an acceptable score under examination conditions but we recommend that you think about having more practice or lessons before you take IELTS.	you are likely to get an acceptable score under examination conditions but remember that different institutions will find different scores acceptable.

TEST 6

LISTENING

Section 1, Questions 1–10

1   2.45
2   band
3   play
4   scientist
5   river
6   grandparents
7   Handsworth
8   traditional
9   outdoor
10   logo

Section 3, Questions 21–30

21   C
22   B
23   C
24   A
25   C
26   E
27   G
28   D
29   C
30   A

Section 2, Questions 11–20

11   B
12   C
13   A
14   B
15   C
16   F
17   B
18   E
19   G
20   C

Section 4, Questions 31–40

31   bullying
32   superiority
33   personality
34   structural
35   absence
36   confidence
37   visions
38   democratic
39   respect
40   mediator

If you score ...

0–16	17–25	26–40
you are unlikely to get an acceptable score under examination conditions and we recommend that you spend a lot of time improving your English before you take IELTS.	you may get an acceptable score under examination conditions but we recommend that you think about having more practice or lessons before you take IELTS.	you are likely to get an acceptable score under examination conditions but remember that different institutions will find different scores acceptable.

READING

Reading Passage 1, Questions 1–14

1 booklet
2 checklist
3 website
4 value
5 (provide) photograph(s) / photos
6 (original) packaging
7 sender
8 A
9 F
10 D
11 B
12 E
13 D
14 E

Reading Passage 2, Questions 15–27

15 indoor (staff/employees)
16 3 weeks/three weeks
17 maternity (leave)
18 5 years/five years
19 pension(s)
20 (registered) psychologists
21 (written) contract
22 qualifications/courses
23 outline/term
24 (prior) coursework
25 (employer's) workforce
26 journey workers
27 location

Reading Passage 3, Questions 28–40

28 vi
29 ix
30 vii
31 iii
32 ii
33 iv
34 viii
35 integrated
36 competition
37 hovercraft(s)
38 piers
39 tunnel
40 concrete

If you score ...

0–20	21–32	33–40
you are unlikely to get an acceptable score under examination conditions and we recommend that you spend a lot of time improving your English before you take IELTS.	you may get an acceptable score under examination conditions but we recommend that you think about having more practice or lessons before you take IELTS.	you are likely to get an acceptable score under examination conditions but remember that different institutions will find different scores acceptable.

TEST 7

LISTENING

Section 1, Questions 1–10

1 travel/travel(l)ing
2 history
3 study
4 teenagers
5 kitchen
6 crime
7 appointment/booking
8 sugar
9 stamps
10 parking

Section 2, Questions 11–20

11&12 *IN EITHER ORDER*
     D
     E
13&14 *IN EITHER ORDER*
     A
     C
15 C
16 B
17 A
18 stress
19 weight
20 families

Section 3, Questions 21–30

21 C
22 E
23 H
24 B
25 A
26 F
27 A
28 C
29 B
30 B

Section 4, Questions 31–40

31 insects
32 behaviour/behavior
33 father
34 complex/complicated
35 reproduction/breeding
36 control
37 duck(s)
38 language
39 food
40 cost(s)/price(s)/bill(s)

If you score ...

0–15	16–25	26–40
you are unlikely to get an acceptable score under examination conditions and we recommend that you spend a lot of time improving your English before you take IELTS.	you may get an acceptable score under examination conditions but we recommend that you think about having more practice or lessons before you take IELTS.	you are likely to get an acceptable score under examination conditions but remember that different institutions will find different scores acceptable.

READING

Reading Passage 1, Questions 1–14

1   C
2   E
3   D
4   B
5   E
6   A
7   C
8   TRUE
9   FALSE
10 NOT GIVEN
11 FALSE
12 TRUE
13 NOT GIVEN
14 TRUE

Reading Passage 2, Questions 15–27

15 contribution
16 sick
17 loans
18 parents
19 policies/schemes

20 parking
21 holidays
22 retain
23 targets
24 commission
25 senior
26 meetings/letters
27 women

Reading Passage 3, Questions 28–40

28 vi
29 iv
30 ii
31 viii
32 v
33 vii
34 iii
35 A
36 C
37 B
38 glaciers
39 birds
40 oxygen

If you score …

0–22	23–32	33–40
you are unlikely to get an acceptable score under examination conditions and we recommend that you spend a lot of time improving your English before you take IELTS.	you may get an acceptable score under examination conditions but we recommend that you think about having more practice or lessons before you take IELTS.	you are likely to get an acceptable score under examination conditions but remember that different institutions will find different scores acceptable.

TEST 8

LISTENING

Section 1, Questions 1–10

1	temporary
2	doctor
3	Africa
4	youth
5	May
6	cheese
7	Arbuthnot
8	DG7 4PH
9	Tuesday
10	talk/presentation

Section 2, Questions 11–20

11	A
12	C
13	B
14	B
15	H
16	C
17	F
18	G
19	I
20	B

Section 3, Questions 21–30

21	classification
22	worst
23	slides
24	issues
25	F
26	A
27	E
28	C
29	G
30	B

Section 4, Questions 31–40

31	garden(s)
32	political
33	work/study
34	fountain
35	social
36	lively
37	training
38	culture
39	nature
40	silent

If you score …

0–15	16–24	25–40
you are unlikely to get an acceptable score under examination conditions and we recommend that you spend a lot of time improving your English before you take IELTS.	you may get an acceptable score under examination conditions but we recommend that you think about having more practice or lessons before you take IELTS.	you are likely to get an acceptable score under examination conditions but remember that different institutions will find different scores acceptable.

READING

Reading Passage 1,
Questions 1–14

1   C
2   A
3   D
4   A
5   B
6   A
7   C
8   D
9   security
10 safety
11 machinery
12 photography
13 nursery
14 accident

Reading Passage 2,
Questions 15–27

15 asset
16 culture
17 internet
18 union
19 review
20 compromise
21 budget
22 scope creep
23 skills
24 (clear) communication
25 (interim) milestones
26 (contingency) plans
27 report

Reading Passage 3,
Questions 28–40

28 D
29 B
30 C
31 FALSE
32 TRUE
33 FALSE
34 TRUE
35 NOT GIVEN
36 FALSE
37 plankton
38 parasites
39 wings
40 brain

If you score …

0–23	24–32	33–40
you are unlikely to get an acceptable score under examination conditions and we recommend that you spend a lot of time improving your English before you take IELTS.	you may get an acceptable score under examination conditions but we recommend that you think about having more practice or lessons before you take IELTS.	you are likely to get an acceptable score under examination conditions but remember that different institutions will find different scores acceptable.

Sample answers for Writing tasks

TEST 5, WRITING TASK 1

SAMPLE ANSWER

This is an answer written by a candidate who achieved a **Band 6.5** score. Here is the examiner's comment:

> The response covers all the requirements of the task, shows a clear purpose and uses an appropriate tone. All the bullet points are well covered. Organisation is logical and there is a clear progression throughout the response. Cohesive devices are used flexibly. The range of vocabulary is sufficient and appropriate for the task, and, although there are errors [*Houman Resourse | hard driver | at least | metters*], the meaning is still clear. There is a mix of simple and complex sentence forms, but complex structures are produced less accurately than simple forms [*I was have many works should finish by yesterday | … I couldn't wait to fix that so long*].

Dear Sir or Madam,

I work as a Houman Resourse manager and I do all my work at home. Few months ago I needed to buy extra hard driver for arrange my all work files. I bought sony 1000GB hard driver from your store in O'connell street in May. I was really happy to use this hd until yesterday. Yesterday morning I started to use work files from hd but was reading so long and at least it stucked I tried turn on and off computer but still same and couldn't open the files.

I was have many works should finish by yesterday. Also all of my meeting appointments files was in that hd but all cancelled because I couldn't see the time and places. Yesterday afternoon I called to your customer service but they explained that I have to wait 3 working days.

I have many urgent metters in this hd so I couldn't wait to fix that so long. This hd have still a guarantee.

I have request to fix this hd and recover all my files by today!

I belive you are good and well known company so I'm waiting for your best and user friendly service as soon as possible.

Thanks and regards

TEST 5, WRITING TASK 2

SAMPLE ANSWER

This is an answer written by a candidate who achieved a **Band 5.0** score. Here is the examiner's comment:

> The candidate focuses on tourists visiting the desert, rather than on visiting places where conditions are difficult, so the prompt is not fully addressed. There is an attempt to discuss some benefits and disadvantages, but ideas are limited. The response is organised into paragraphs, but the focus of each is not always clear, while cohesive devices are sometimes faulty [*as compare to*] and the subject of reference pronouns is sometimes ambiguous [*Although the conditions are a bit more difficult in such type of places but they are excited… | The benefits to visit such areas is that they actually want to …*]. The range of lexis is sometimes limited [*The people discovering the things*], yet the candidate is quite adventurous at times [*some research about how to survive in deserts | cannel of water | depth | deep | casualty rate*]. There are attempts to produce complex structures, but these usually contain errors [*what is the reasons for that | Although … but | Here is another example that …*].

The globalization is the most important topic for all the people. They want to know what is happening around and what is the reasons for that. The people discovering the things and geting well aware about hiden things. The tourists are visiting the deserts more as compare to other places. Although the conditions are bit more difficult in such type of places but they are excited to know about each and everything.

The benefits to visit such areas is that they actually want to let people know what is the difference between the life in desert and other normal places. It is shown in one of the australian movie which is cast on a Japanese. In movie the Japese goes to desert for some research about how to survive in deserts. His car stuck into the desert. He just keeps try to get out of there and at the end he become succeed. After moving forward some distance he watch a cannel of water and he jump into that water but depth is not so much and he dies because his neck hit by stone into the water. So it make us realize that when you found a cannel in deserts especially first make sure that how deep it is.

ISecondly, the disadvantages to visit the deserts is that the casualty rate is more in deserts as compare to other discoveries. When tourists go to the desert, they even don't know either they will return back to home or not.

The case is that the people are going to desert more because there are more things to discover like mines, minerals, medical related preventions etc. Here is another example that once people got diamonds from desert which was in UAE. They took it as pebbles but when they came back to home they realize that were diamonds.

TEST 6, WRITING TASK 1

SAMPLE ANSWER

This is an answer written by a candidate who achieved a **Band 6.0** score. Here is the examiner's comment:

> The purpose of the letter is clear, but the tone is not entirely consistent [*Dear Sir / I am not working at the moment and I need some money*]. All three bullet points are covered quite well, however. Information and ideas are arranged coherently and there is a clear overall progression, with sufficient use of cohesive devices. The range of lexis is adequate and appropriate for the task [*I really want to work in your chain of restaurant*(s) | *working … as a chef* | *experience working with other people* | *consider my application*]. Spelling is generally accurate. There is a mix of simple and complex sentence forms, and grammatical control is generally accurate.

Dear Sir,

I am Alejandro Garcia, we met last week in a plane journey from London to Manchester. I am writing to tell you that I really want to work in your chain of restaurant because I am not working at the moment and I need some money.

In my last two years I had been working in restaurant as a chef and I have been doing an Indian and an Italian course in a very famous academy. So if I had to choose I would like to be the chef. However, if you already have chefs I wouldn't have problem to work as a waiter

I think I will be suitable for this job because I am a very responsible person and I have been training very hard to have a possibility like this. Also, I have experience working with other people and how to manage a group.

I hope you would consider my application. I look forward to hearing from you soon.

Yours faithfully

Alejandro Garcia

TEST 6, WRITING TASK 2

SAMPLE ANSWER

This is an answer written by a candidate who achieved a **Band 7.0** score. Here is the examiner's comment:

> This is a well-organised piece of writing, presenting ideas on both sides of the debate, developing these ideas effectively and also showing the candidate's own position throughout the response. Ideas are logically organised and there is a clear progression in the train of thought. Each paragraph has a clear central topic, which is developed, and there is effective use of cohesive devices. The lexical resource is sufficient to allow some flexibility and precision and there is use of less common items [*natural ecosystem | human settlement | engineering projects | the most extreme supporters of | in harmony with surrounding nature*]. There are occasional errors in spelling and collocation [*prominance | heavy debates | go extinct*], but these do not detract from overall clarity. There is a variety of complex structures, used with flexibility and accuracy, while grammar and punctuation are generally well controlled. Errors do not adversely affect the overall message.

Presently, the problem of a living space has risen into prominance in many places of the country. There is absolutely no way to build new houses in some cities, and a lot of people suggest to carry out construction in the countryside. However, it is a controversial topic introducing heavy debates.

Opponents of urbanisation of former rural areas state that it would cause a dramatic effect on the natural ecosystem of such places. The most drastic consequences are caused by infrastructure that necessarily follows any human settlement – that is, roads, power lines, means of water supply and such. The construction of those engineering projects leads to destruction of natural bioms of ponds, rivers and forests, causing many animals to migrate or go extinct. The arguments of environmentalists do make sense, but there also valuable ideas supporting the countryside occupation.

First of all, not even the most extreme supporters of spreading urbanization maintain that all of the countryside should be filled with homes all over the place. In fact, there are good examples of even larger cities living perhaps not in harmony with surrounding nature, but at least in some form of cooperation. Having a considerable amounts of parks inside inhabited area help both people to feel themselves better and plants and animals to have some sort of home. If I may to present an example, the city of Zaporizhia where I live has a large island between the parts of the city which is covered with trees and largely unoccupied, being a nice counterpart to heavily populated nearby districts.

In conclusion, I would like to stress that while opponents of countryside settlements have many valid points, the situation is not as drastic as they portray it, and the co-existence of human population with nature is quite possible.

TEST 7, WRITING TASK 1

SAMPLE ANSWER

This is an answer written by a candidate who achieved a **Band 5.0** score. Here is the examiner's comment:

> The response addresses all three bullet points, but the ideas that are presented show little development. The purpose of the letter is clear, however, and the writer's position is given at the end. Information is presented with some organisation and some basic linking devices are used [*Firstly* | *Secondly* | *In fact*]; there are also examples of simple reference words [*this team* | *This solution* | *this case*]. The writer would need to use a wider range of cohesive devices to achieve a higher score here. There are attempts to use a range of vocabulary [*obtain* | *advertising campain*/campaign | *maximum savety*/safety | *alhcolic*/alcoholic *beverage*/s | *in according*/accordance *with the Council*], but these usually show errors in spelling or word formation. Other errors could cause some comprehension problems [*sctisfect*/satisfied? | *challenging*/competitions? | *sujection*/subject? possibility? proposal? | *reguilty*?]. There are attempts to use complex sentences [*I would explain in witch ways, you'll be obtain …* | *sponsoring a sport children team* | *We could mixte with… when the team need…*], but the level of error is high and can cause some difficulty for the reader.

Dear Sir or Madam,

According to your letter, I'm very grateful and sctisfect, by you confidence. I would explain in witch ways, you'll be obtain a good feedback from the general public.

Firstly, sponsoring a sport children team could increase the numbers of visitors (for examples, family, friends), and also the level of this team, and check the place too. We could mixte with an advertising campain when the team need to move for challenging.

Secondly, we have another sujection it's create two open-air concerts. This solution have a big advantage, because a lot of range of people could beneficited.

We can offer a large range of free item included. But it's this case we reguilty a maximum savety of people to controlled the side and avoid alhcolic beverage. It's very huge risk for evrything and we need to have in according with the Council.

In fact, I prefered to give my advice for this sponsorised local children, is very a good mark for the community and for the further customers.

I'm wainting you respond sooner, and I'll hope to expose dearly my wiev point.

Best regards,

Sample answers for Writing tasks

TEST 7, WRITING TASK 2

SAMPLE ANSWER

This is an answer written by a candidate who achieved a **Band 6.0** score. Here is the examiner's comment:

> The response addresses all parts of the prompt, although the idea that children should learn how to occupy themselves on their own is not as fully explored as the first part of the prompt. Even here the candidate only mentions educational activities organised by teachers: a stronger response might consider other types of organised activities, such as sports teams, dance or orchestral groups, which could develop other aspects of a child's growth. Ideas are organised, however, and there is a clear overall progression. There is some effective use of signalling devices [*However* | *On the one hand* | *On the other hand* | *For instance* | *To sum up*] and other examples of cohesive devices are also used [*such events* | *during this time*]. Paragraphing is signalled, though not consistently. The range of vocabulary is quite wide and shows awareness of collocation [*participate in group activities* | *schedule their time* | *current generation* | *give them permission to* | *encouraged to attend* | *in certain circumstances* | *spare time* | *supervise children*], but there are rather too many errors for a higher band here [*intellegent* | *possitive* | *throght*/through | *destinguish* | *recieve*]. The use of [*kids*], repeated twice as [*kinds*] is not appropriate in this type of response. There is a mix of simple and complex sentence forms and although errors occur, they rarely reduce communication.

In today's world many people tend to believe that children should better participate in group activities that organised with certain purpose by teachers or their parent. However, others do not agree and suggest that kids become more intellegent whilst occupy themselves as in their future lives children will have to schedule their time.

On the one hand, I must admit that teachers have much more experience and knowledge in how to amuse pupils and provide them with some useful education at the same time. In this case society can count on school workers as they help to bring up good change for current generation. Parents should give them permission to occupy their children's free time with organised group activities and provide all possible help. Children have to be encouraged to attend in such events as it have possitive contribution in their studying process.

On the other hand, in certain circumstances parents should let their children to plan part of their spare time by themselves. For instance, kinds have to be wise about how to schedule their time at the evening when no other activities are available. But still parents should supervise children during this time in order to not let them play video games all night throght.

To sum up it is important to notice that children in their young ages are not so self-confident and intellegent to destingush what is useful for them and what is not. That is why teachers parents should always participate in activities which kinds involved in. To help them recieve more useful knowledge during their childhood.

TEST 8, WRITING TASK 1

SAMPLE ANSWER

This is an answer written by a candidate who achieved a **Band 7.0** score. Here is the examiner's comment:

> The letter opens with a clear statement of purpose and goes on to address each bullet point, covering the first and the third at some length. There is room for expansion of the second bullet point. Information and ideas are logically organised, following the bullet points, and there is a clear progression throughout the response. There is a range of linking devices [*as well as | due to | What is more | In addition | which leads to | Needless to say | Taking everything into consideration | Moreover | Finally*], although not all of these are strictly necessary. There is evidence of less common vocabulary [*outline | improvements | implemented | spacious | overcrowded | beneficial | advantageous*] and use of collocations [*expressed their dissatisfaction | image of a company | first impression*]. There are only occasional spelling errors [*reseptionist | equipt | sesirelly*], but the meaning is always clear (the position of [*sesirelly*] makes it clear that [sincerely] was intended). A variety of complex grammatical structures is used flexibly, while control over grammar and punctuation is good, apart from the use of a full stop rather than a comma in the phrase [*area.due to the fact that*].

Dear Mr Smith,

I am writing to outline the complaints that have been made about the reception area as well as to suggest several improvements to be implemented.

A number of visitors expressed their dissatisfaction with our company's reception area. due to the fact that it is not spacious and overcrowded. What is more, there are not enough desks to fill in the various forms. In addition, only one reseptionist can be addressed to with a great number of questions which leads to the place being overcrowded.

Needless to say, the area where visitors arrive is extremely important as it is the image of a company and gives the first impression about the organization.

Taking everything into consideration, it is highly recommended to widen the reception area by using the room next to it

Moreover, it would be beneficial to equipt the place with additional furniture for visitors to use. Finally, hiring a second receptionist would be definitely advantageous.

I am looking forward to the changes being implemented.

Yours sesirelly,

TEST 8, WRITING TASK 2

SAMPLE ANSWER

This is an answer written by a candidate who achieved a **Band 5.0** score. Here is the examiner's comment:

> The candidate identifies some positive and negative aspects of the topic, but does not offer any conclusion, which weakens the effectiveness of the response. The ideas presented are not always developed and or relevant ([*celebrities making marketing with this products | local shops may be big factories in the future*]). Ideas are organised into paragraphs and there is some use of linking devices [*Nowadays | Ussually | that's why | instead of | all of this*], but there is a lack of overall progression because there is no conclusion. There is some good use of vocabulary [*outlet | popular stores | local shops | promotions*], but spelling errors are noticeable [*differents | Ussually | demande | diarectly | you/your home | clossing*]. Errors in word formation also occur [*exportation | this/these shops*] and there is first language influence in the use of [*Fabric*] instead of [*factory*] which could cause some comprehension problems. There are attempts to use complex sentences, but errors in grammar and punctuation are frequent. The punctuation errors can cause some difficulty for the reader.

Nowadays there are differents ways to buy clothes, but it is known that people love to go shopping, the problem is that some store that are near to our home doesn't have the clothes we like, so we need to go far away to a big outlet, where we can find popular stores even if we have local shops with quality clothes.

Ussually the big stores are popular because the demande of the products that's why the Fabrics are outside the cities, IF you go diarectly to a Fabric it is easier For you to find a promotions or products that are more cheap, instead of going to a store that is close to you home where, sometimes it is more expensive because they bring the clothes and the transportation or if we are talking about an international product the exportation. Most of the people prefer to save some money going to the principal store.

The negative aspect of all of this is that a lot of local shops are clossing, thats why they are creating projects that help this local stores, some companies are investing in this shops by putting them a lot of marketing that help the shops to be popular and Famous, this is really helping the shops, a lot of celebrities and famous people are making marketing with this products and making them a popular product. So now this local shops may be big factories in the future.

Sample answer sheets

BRITISH COUNCIL **idp** IELTS AUSTRALIA **CAMBRIDGE ENGLISH** Language Assessment — Part of the University of Cambridge

IELTS Listening and Reading Answer Sheet

Centre number:

Pencil must be used to complete this sheet.

0 1 2 3 4 5 6 7 8 9
0 1 2 3 4 5 6 7 8 9
0 1 2 3 4 5 6 7 8 9
0 1 2 3 4 5 6 7 8 9
0 1 2 3 4 5 6 7 8 9
0 1 2 3 4 5 6 7 8 9

Please write your **full name** in CAPITAL letters on the line below.

SAMPLE

Then write your six digit Candidate number in the boxes and shade the number in the grid on the right.

Test date (shade ONE box for the day, ONE box for the month and ONE box for the year):

Day: 01 02 03 04 05 06 07 08 09 10 11 12 13 14 15 16 17 18 19 20 21 22 23 24 25 26 27 28 29 30 31

Month: 01 02 03 04 05 06 07 08 09 10 11 12   **Year** (last 2 digits): 13 14 15 16 17 18 19 20 21

	Listening			Marker use only		Listening			Marker use only
1				✓ 1 ✗	21				✓ 21 ✗
2				✓ 2 ✗	22				✓ 22 ✗
3				✓ 3 ✗	23				✓ 23 ✗
4				✓ 4 ✗	24				✓ 24 ✗
5				✓ 5 ✗	25				✓ 25 ✗
6				✓ 6 ✗	26				✓ 26 ✗
7				✓ 7 ✗	27				✓ 27 ✗
8				✓ 8 ✗	28				✓ 28 ✗
9				✓ 9 ✗	29				✓ 29 ✗
10				✓ 10 ✗	30				✓ 30 ✗
11				✓ 11 ✗	31				✓ 31 ✗
12				✓ 12 ✗	32				✓ 32 ✗
13				✓ 13 ✗	33				✓ 33 ✗
14				✓ 14 ✗	34				✓ 34 ✗
15				✓ 15 ✗	35				✓ 35 ✗
16				✓ 16 ✗	36				✓ 36 ✗
17				✓ 17 ✗	37				✓ 37 ✗
18				✓ 18 ✗	38				✓ 38 ✗
19				✓ 19 ✗	39				✓ 39 ✗
20				✓ 20 ✗	40				✓ 40 ✗

Marker 2 Signature   Marker 1 Signature   Listening Total

IELTS L-R v1.0   denote Print Limited 0121 520 5100   DP787/394

Sample answer sheets

Please write your **full name** in CAPITAL letters on the line below:

SAMPLE

Please write your Candidate number on the line below:

Please write your three digit language code in the boxes and shade the numbers in the grid on the right.

0 1 2 3 4 5 6 7 8 9
0 1 2 3 4 5 6 7 8 9
0 1 2 3 4 5 6 7 8 9

Are you: Female? ⎯ Male? ⎯

Reading   Reading   Reading   Reading   Reading   Reading

Module taken (shade one box): Academic ⎯   General Training ⎯

	Marker use only				Marker use only
1	✓ 1 ✗	**21**		✓ 21 ✗
2	✓ 2 ✗	**22**		✓ 22 ✗
3	✓ 3 ✗	**23**		✓ 23 ✗
4	✓ 4 ✗	**24**		✓ 24 ✗
5	✓ 5 ✗	**25**		✓ 25 ✗
6	✓ 6 ✗	**26**		✓ 26 ✗
7	✓ 7 ✗	**27**		✓ 27 ✗
8	✓ 8 ✗	**28**		✓ 28 ✗
9	✓ 9 ✗	**29**		✓ 29 ✗
10	✓ 10 ✗	**30**		✓ 30 ✗
11	✓ 11 ✗	**31**		✓ 31 ✗
12	✓ 12 ✗	**32**		✓ 32 ✗
13	✓ 13 ✗	**33**		✓ 33 ✗
14	✓ 14 ✗	**34**		✓ 34 ✗
15	✓ 15 ✗	**35**		✓ 35 ✗
16	✓ 16 ✗	**36**		✓ 36 ✗
17	✓ 17 ✗	**37**		✓ 37 ✗
18	✓ 18 ✗	**38**		✓ 38 ✗
19	✓ 19 ✗	**39**		✓ 39 ✗
20	✓ 20 ✗	**40**		✓ 40 ✗

Marker 2 Signature		Marker 1 Signature		Reading Total

BRITISH COUNCIL **idp** IELTS AUSTRALIA **CAMBRIDGE ENGLISH** Language Assessment Part of the University of Cambridge

IELTS Writing Answer Sheet – TASK 1

Candidate Name

Centre Number

Candidate Number

Module (shade one box):   Academic ▭   General Training ▭

Test date

D D   M M   Y Y Y Y

TASK 1

Do not write below this line

100913/2

BRITISH COUNCIL

idp
IELTS AUSTRALIA

CAMBRIDGE ENGLISH
Language Assessment
Part of the University of Cambridge

IELTS Writing Answer Sheet – TASK 2

Candidate Name

Centre Number

Candidate Number

Module (shade one box): Academic ☐ General Training ☐

Test date

D D M M Y Y Y Y

TASK 2

Do not write below this line

100895/2

Acknowledgements

The authors and publishers acknowledge the following sources of copyright material and are grateful for the permissions granted. While every effort has been made, it has not always been possible to identify the sources of all the material used, or to trace all copyright holders. If any omissions are brought to our notice, we will be happy to include the appropriate acknowledgements on reprinting and in the next update to the digital edition, as applicable.

Text on p. 16 adapted from "Across the network from 'Go to'... First Great Western free magazine". Copyright © Great Western Railway. Reproduced with kind permission; Text on p. 18 adapted from 'About big rock'. Copyright © Big Rock Climbing Centre. Reproduced with kind permission of Big Rock Climbing Centre (www.bigrockclimbing.com); Text on p. 20 adapted from 'How to get hold of more customers'. Copyright © hibu (UK) Limited. Reproduced with kind permission of Yell; Robert Addams for the text on pp. 24–25 adapted from 'Automata'. Reproduced with kind permission of Robert Addams; Text on pp. 24–25 adapted from 'A Pleasure for the Archbishop. The trick fountains machinery at the Summer Palace at Hellbrunn' by Katharina Müller-Uri. Reproduced with permission of Katharina Müller-Uri; Text on p. 38 adapted from 'Lost, Damaged or Delayed Inland Mail Claim Form'. Copyright © 2014 Royal Mail Group Ltd. Reproduced with kind permission; Text on p. 40 adapted from 'Let's Go Out Volkswagen Touron family guide'. Copyright © Volkswagen UK. Reproduced with kind permission; Text on p. 42 adapted from 'Staff Benefits & Working Conditions'. Copyright © North Sydney Council. Reproduced with kind permission; Text on p. 44 adapted from 'Become an Apprentice'. Copyright © New York State Department of Labor. Reproduced with kind permission of New York State Department of Labor; Text on pp. 46–47 adapted from 'How we made the Humber Bridge' interview by Dave Simpson. Copyright © 2016 Guardian News & Media Ltd. Reproduced with permission; Text on pp. 46–47 adapted from 'The Ferry'. Copyright © The Humber Bridge Board. Reproduced with kind permission; Text on pp. 59–60 adapted from 'Education courses'. Copyright © City College Brighton and Hove. Reproduced with kind permission; Text on pp. 62–63 adapted from 'Maintenance training'. Copyright © Birmingham Bike Foundry Ltd. Reproduced with permission; Text on pp. 72–74 adapted from 'Marine ecosystem'. Copyright © 2007 *Geographical Magazine*. Reproduced with permission; Text on p. 90 adapted from 'Acceptance and rejection: Negotiating a better package for your new job'. Copyright © GTI Media Ltd. Reproduced with kind permission of targetjobs.co.uk; Text on p. 92–93 adapted from 'A Manager's 7 Tips for a Successful Project' by Simon Andras. Copyright © lifehack.org. Reproduced with kind permission; Text on pp. 95–96 adapted from 'Maldives: diving with manta rays' by Tim Ecott. Copyright © Telegraph Media Group Limited 2011. Reproduced with permission; Text on pp. 102–103 adapted from 'Walter Peak Guided Cycling'. Copyright © Real Journeys 2017. Reproduced with kind permission; Text on pp. 105–106 adapted from 'Sacred Cow or Trojan Horse?' by Ben Walker. Copyright © 2015 CMI's Insights web channel at managers.org.uk/insights. Reproduced with kind permission of Chartered Management Institute; Text on pp. 111–112 adapted from 'Fight the good fight- Professional Manager, Summer 2013'. Copyright © 2013 CMI's Insights web channel at managers.org.uk/insights. Reproduced with kind permission of Chartered Management Institute; Text on pp. 113–114 adapted from 'The Consumer Holiday Trends Report ABTA Consumer Survey 2013'. Copyright © ABTA Ltd. Reproduced with kind permission; Text on pp. 113–114 adapted from 'About our Fitness Holidays'. Copyright © Health and Fitness Travel Ltd. Reproduced with kind permission; Text on pp. 116–117 adapted from 'Mercury hurts birds and people: what we can learn from studying our feathered friends' by Jenny R. Isaacs, interview by Claire Varian-Ramos. Reproduced with permission of Mongabay.com.